I0752622

THE WANDERING JEW

BOOK II

Eugene Sue

The Wandering Jew, Book II

Eugene Sue

© 1st World Library, 2006
PO Box 2211
Fairfield, IA 52556
www.1stworldlibrary.com
First Edition

LCCN: 2006935218

Softcover ISBN: 1-4218-2471-X
Hardcover ISBN: 1-4218-2371-3
eBook ISBN: 1-4218-2571-6

Purchase *"The Wandering Jew, Book II"*
as a traditional bound book at:
www.1stWorldLibrary.com/purchase.asp?ISBN=1-4218-2471-X

1st World Library is a literary, educational organization dedicated to:

- Creating a free internet library of downloadable ebooks
- Hosting writing competitions and offering book publishing scholarships.

Interested in more 1st World Library books?
contact: literacy@1stworldlibrary.com
Check us out at: www.1stworldlibrary.com

1st World Library Literary Society

Giving Back to the World

"If you want to work on the core problem, it's early school literacy."

- James Barksdale, former CEO of Netscape

"No skill is more crucial to the future of a child, or to a democratic and prosperous society, than literacy."

- Los Angeles Times

Literacy... means far more than learning how to read and write... The aim is to transmit... knowledge and promote social participation."

- UNESCO

"Literacy is not a luxury, it is a right and a responsibility. If our world is to meet the challenges of the twenty-first century we must harness the energy and creativity of all our citizens."

- President Bill Clinton

"Parents should be encouraged to read to their children, and teachers should be equipped with all available techniques for teaching literacy, so the varying needs and capacities of individual kids can be taken into account."

- Hugh Mackay

CONTENTS

BOOK II

INTERVAL

THE WANDERING JEW'S SENTENCE

The site is wild and rugged. It is a lofty eminence covered with huge boulders of sandstone, between which rise birch trees and oaks, their foliage already yellowed by autumn. These tall trees stand out from the background of red light, which the sun has left in the west, resembling the reflection of a great fire.

From this eminence the eye looks down into a deep valley, shady, fertile, and half-veiled in light vapor by the evening mist. The rich meadows, the tufts of bushy trees the fields from which the ripe corn has been gathered in, all blend together in one dark, uniform tint, which contrasts with the limpid azure of the heavens. Steeples of gray stone or slate lift their pointed spires, at intervals, from the midst of this valley; for many villages are spread about it, bordering a high-road which leads from the north to the west.

It is the hour of repose - the hour when, for the most part, every cottage window brightens to the joyous crackling of the rustic hearth, and shines afar through shade and foliage, whilst clouds of smoke issue from the chimneys, and curl up slowly towards the sky. But now, strange to say, every hearth in the country seems cold and deserted. Stranger and more fatal still, every steeple rings out a funeral knell. Whatever there is of activity, movement, or life, appears concentrated in that lugubrious and far-sounding vibration.

Lights begin to show themselves in the dark villages, but they rise not from the cheerful and pleasant rustic hearth. They are as red as the fires of the herdsmen, seen at night through the midst of the fog. And then these lights do not remain motionless. They creep slowly towards the churchyard of every village. Louder sounds the death-knell, the air trembles beneath the strokes of so many bells, and, at rare intervals, the funeral chant rises faintly to the summit of the hill.

Why so many interments? What valley of desolation is this, where the peaceful songs which follow the hard labors of the day are replaced by the death dirge? where the repose of evening is exchanged for the repose of eternity? What is this valley of the shadow, where every village mourns for its many dead, and buries them at the same hour of the same night?

Alas! the deaths are so sudden and numerous and frightful that there is hardly time to bury the dead. During day the survivors are chained to the earth by hard but necessary toil; and only in the evening, when they return from the fields, are they able, though sinking with fatigue, to dig those other furrows, in which their brethren are to lie heaped like grains of corn.

And this valley is not the only one that has seen the desolation. During a series of fatal years, many villages, many towns, many cities, many great countries, have seen, like this valley, their hearths deserted and cold - have seen, like this valley, mourning take the place of joy, and the death-knell substituted for the noise of festival - have wept in the same day for their many dead, and buried them at night by the lurid glare of torches.

For, during those fatal years, an awful wayfarer had slowly journeyed over the earth, from one pole to the other - from the depths of India and Asia to the ice of Siberia - from the ice of Siberia to the borders of the seas of France.

This traveller, mysterious as death, slow as eternity, implacable as fate, terrible as the hand of heaven, was the CHOLERA!

The tolling of bells and the funeral chants still rose from the depths of the valley to the summit of the hill, like the complaining of a mighty voice; the glare of the funeral torches was still seen afar through the mist of evening; it was the hour of twilight - that strange hour, which gives to the most solid forms a vague, indefinite fantastic appearance - when the sound of firm and regular footsteps was heard on the stony soil of the rising ground, and, between the black trunks of the trees, a man passed slowly onward.

His figure was tall, his head was bowed upon his breast; his countenance was noble, gentle, and sad; his eyebrows, uniting in the midst, extended from one temple to the other, like a fatal mark on his forehead.

This man did not seem to hear the distant tolling of so many funeral bells - and yet, a few days before, repose and happiness, health and joy, had reigned in those villages through which he had slowly passed, and which he now left behind him, mourning and desolate. But the traveller continued on his way, absorbed in his own reflections.

"The 13th of February approaches," thought he; "the day approaches, in which the descendants of my beloved sister, the last scions of our race, should meet in Paris. Alas! it is now a hundred and fifty years since, for the third time, persecution scattered this family over all the earth - this family, that I have watched over with tenderness for eighteen centuries, through all its migrations and exiles, its changes of religion, fortune, and name!

"Oh! for this family, descended from the sister of the poor shoemaker,[2] what grandeur and what abasement, what obscurity and what splendor, what misery and what glory! By how many crimes has it been sullied, by how many virtues honored! The history of this single family is the history of the human race!

"Passing, in the course of so many generations, through the

veins of the poor and the rich, of the sovereign and the bandit, of the wise man and the fool, of the coward and the brave, of the saint and the atheist, the blood of my sister has transmitted itself to this hour.

"What scions of this family are now remaining? Seven only.

"Two orphans, the daughters of proscribed parents - a dethroned prince - a poor missionary priest - a man of the middle class - a young girl of a great name and large fortune - a mechanic.

"Together, they comprise in themselves the virtues, the courage, the degradation, the splendor, the miseries of our species!

"Siberia - India - America - France - behold the divers places where fate has thrown them!

"My instinct teaches me when one of them is in peril. Then, from the North to the South, from the East to the West, I go to seek them. Yesterday amid the polar frosts - to-day in the temperate zone - to-morrow beneath the fires of the tropics - but often, alas! at the moment when my presence might save them, the invisible hand impels me, the whirlwind carries me away, and the voice speaks in my ear: 'GO ON! GO ON!'

"Oh, that I might only finish my task! - 'GO ON!' - A single hour - only a single hour of repose! - 'GO ON!' - Alas! I leave those I love on the brink of the abyss! - 'GO ON! GO ON!'

"Such is my punishment. If it is great, my crime was greater still! An artisan, devoted to privations and misery, my misfortunes had made me cruel.

"Oh, cursed, cursed be the day, when, as I bent over my work, sullen with hate and despair, because, in spite of my incessant labor, I and mine wanted for everything, the Saviour passed before my door.

"Reviled, insulted, covered with blows, hardly able to sustain the weight of his heavy cross, He asked me to let Him rest a moment on my stone bench. The sweat poured from His forehead, His feet were bleeding, He was well-nigh sinking with fatigue, and He said to me, in a mild, heart piercing voice: 'I suffer!' 'And I too suffer,' I replied, as with harsh anger I pushed Him from the place; 'I suffer, and no one comes to help me! I find no pity, and will give none. Go on! go on!' Then, with a deep sigh of pain, He answered, and spake this sentence: 'Verily, thou shalt go on till the day of thy redemption, for so wills the Father which art in heaven!'

"And so my punishment began. Too late I opened these eyes to the light, too late I learned repentance and charity, too late I understood those divine words of Him I had outraged, words which should be the law of the whole human race. 'LOVE YE ONE ANOTHER.'

"In vain through successive ages, gathering strength and eloquence from those celestial words, have I labored to earn my pardon, by filling with commiseration and love hearts that were overflowing with envy and bitterness, by inspiring many a soul with a sacred horror of oppression and injustice. For me the day of mercy has not yet dawned!

"And even as the first man, by his fall, devoted his posterity to misfortune, it would seem as if I, the workman, had consigned the whole race of artisans to endless sorrows, and as if they were expiating my crime: for they alone, during these eighteen centuries, have not yet been delivered.

"For eighteen centuries, the powerful and the happy of this world have said to the toiling people what I said to the imploring and suffering Saviour: 'Go on! go on!' And the people, sinking with fatigue, bearing their heavy cross, have answered in the bitterness of their grief: 'Oh, for pity's sake! a few moments of repose; we are worn out with toil.' - Go on!' - 'And if we perish in our pain, what will become of our little children and our aged mothers?' - 'Go on! go on!' And, for eighteen centuries, they and I have continued to struggle forward and to suffer, and no charitable voice has yet pronounced the word 'Enough!'

"Alas! such is my punishment. It is immense, it is two-fold. I suffer in the name of humanity, when I see these wretched multitudes consigned without respite to profitless and oppressive toil. I suffer in the name of my family, when, poor and wandering, I am unable to bring aid to the descendants of my dear sister. But, when the sorrow is above my strength, when I foresee some danger from which I cannot preserve my own, then my thoughts, travelling over the world, go in search of that woman like me accursed, that daughter of a queen, who, like me, the son of a laborer, wanders, and will wander on, till the day of her redemption.[3]

"Once in a century, as two planets draw nigh to each other in their revolutions, I am permitted to meet this woman during the dread week of the Passion. And after this interview, filled with terrible remembrances and boundless griefs, wandering stars of eternity, we pursue our infinite course.

"And this woman, the only one upon earth who, like me, sees the end of every century, and exclaims: 'What another?' this woman responds to my thought, from the furthest extremity of the world. She, who alone shares my terrible destiny, has chosen to share also the only interest that has consoled me for so many ages. Those descendants of my dear sister, she too loves, she too protects them. For them she journeys likewise from East to West and from North to South.

"But alas! the invisible hand impels her, the whirlwind carries her away, and the voice speaks in her ear: 'Go on!' - 'Oh that I might finish my sentence!' repeats she also, - 'Go on!' - 'A single hour - only a single hour of repose!' - Go on!' - 'I leave those I love on the brink of the abyss.' - 'Go on! Go on! -'"

Whilst this man thus went over the hill absorbed in his thoughts, the light evening breeze increased almost to a gale, a vivid flash streamed across the sky, and long, deep whistlings announced the coming of a tempest.

On a sudden this doomed man, who could no longer weep or smile, started with a shudder. No physical pain could reach him, and yet he pressed his hand hastily to his heart, as though he had experienced a cruel pang. "Oh!" cried he; "I feel it. This hour, many of those whom I love - the descendants of my dear sister - suffer, and are in great peril. Some in the centre of India - some in America - some here in Germany. The struggle recommences, the detestable passions are again awake. Oh, thou that hearest me - thou, like myself wandering and accursed - Herodias! help me to protect them! May my invocation reach thee, in those American solitudes where thou now lingerest - and may we arrive in time!"

Thereon an extraordinary event happened. Night was come. The man made a movement; precipitately, to retrace his steps - but an invisible force prevented him, and carried him forward in the opposite direction.

At this moment, the storm burst forth in its murky majesty. One of those whirlwinds, which tear up trees by the roots and shake the foundations of the rocks, rushed over the hill rapid and loud as thunder.

In the midst of the roaring of the hurricane, by the glare of the fiery flashes, the man with the black mark on his brow was seen descending the hill, stalking with huge strides among the rocks, and between trees bent beneath the efforts of the storm.

The tread of this man was no longer slow, firm, and steady - but painfully irregular, like that of one impelled by an irresistible power, or carried along by the whirl of a frightful wind. In vain he extended his supplicating hands to heaven. Soon he disappeared in the shades of night, and amid the roar of the tempest.

[2] It is known that, according to the legend, the Wandering

Jew was a shoemaker at Jerusalem. The Saviour, carrying his cross, passed before the house of the artisan, and asked him to be allowed to rest an instant on the stone bench at his door. "Go on! go on!" said the Jew harshly, pushing him away. "Thou shalt go on till the end of time," answered the Saviour, in a stern though sorrowful tone. For further details, see the eloquent and learned notice by Charles Magnin, appended to the magnificent poem "Ahasuerus," by Ed. Quinet. - E. S.

[3] According to a legend very little known, for we are indebted to the kindness of M. Maury, the learned sub-librarian of the Institute, Herodias was condemned to wander till the day of judgement, for having asked for the death of John the Baptist - E. S.

CHAPTER XVII

THE AJOUPA

While Rodin despatched his cosmopolite correspondence, from his retreat in the Rue du Milieu des Ursins, in Paris - while the daughters of General Simon, after quitting as fugitives the White Falcon, were detained prisoners at Leipsic along with Dagobert - other scenes, deeply interesting to these different personages, were passing, almost as it were at the same moment, at the other extremity of the world, in the furthermost parts of Asia - that is to say, in the island of Java, not far from the city of Batavia, the residence of M. Joshua Van Dael, one of the correspondents of Rodin.

Java! magnificent and fatal country, where the most admirable flowers conceal hideous reptiles, where the brightest fruits contain subtle poisons, where grow splendid trees, whose very shadow is death - where the gigantic vampire bat sucks the blood of its victims whilst it prolongs their sleep, by surrounding them with a fresh and balmy air, no fan moving so rapidly as the great perfumed wings of this monster!

The month of October, 1831, draws near its close. It is noon - an hour well nigh mortal to him who encounters the fiery heat of the sun, which spreads a sheet of dazzling light over the deep blue enamel of the sky.

An ajoupa, or hut, made of cane mats, suspended from long bamboos, which are driven far into the ground, rises in the midst of the bluish shadows cast by a tuft of trees, whose glittering verdure resembles green porcelain. These quaintly formed trees, rounded into arches, pointing like spires, overspreading like parasols, are so thick in foliage, so entangled one with the other, that their dome is impenetrable to the rain.

The soil, ever marshy, notwithstanding the insupportable heat, disappears beneath an inextricable mass of creepers, ferns, and tufted reeds, of a freshness and vigor of vegetation almost incredible, reaching nearly to the top of the ajoupa, which lies hid like a nest among the grass.

Nothing can be more suffocating than the atmosphere, heavily laden with moist exhalations like the steam of hot water, and impregnated with the strongest and sharpest scents; for the cinnamon-tree, ginger-plant, stephanotis and Cape jasmine, mixed with these trees and creepers, spread around in puffs their penetrating odors. A roof, formed of large Indian fig-leaves, covers the cabin; at one end is a square opening, which serves for a window, shut in with a fine lattice-work of vegetable fibres, so as to prevent the reptiles and venomous insects from creeping into the ajoupa. The huge trunk of a dead tree, still standing, but much bent, and with its summit reaching to the roof of the ajoupa, rises from the midst of the brushwood. From every crevice in its black, rugged, mossy bark, springs a strange, almost fantastic flower; the wing of a butterfly is not of a finer tissue, of a more brilliant purple, of a more glossy black: those unknown birds we see in our dreams, have no more grotesque forms than these specimens of the orchis - winged flowers, that seem always ready to fly from their frail and leafless stalks. The long, flexible stems of the cactus, which might be taken for reptiles, encircle also this trunk, and clothe it with their bunches of silvery white, shaded inside with bright orange. These flowers emit a strong scent of vanilla.

A serpent, of a brick-red, about the thickness of a large quill, and five or six inches long, half protrudes its flat head from one of those enormous, perfumed calyces, in which it lies closely curled up.

Within the ajoupa, a young man is extended on a mat in a profound sleep. His complexion of a clear golden yellow, gives him the appearance of a statue of pale bronze, on which a ray of sun is playing. His attitude is simple and graceful; his right arm sustains his head, a little raised and turned on one side; his ample robe of white muslin, with hanging sleeves, leaves uncovered his chest and arms worthy of the Antoinous. Marble is not more firm, more polished than his skin, the golden hue of which contracts strongly with the whiteness of his garments. Upon his broad manly chest a deep scar is visible - the mark of the musket-ball he received in defending the life of General Simon, the father of Rose and Blanche.

Suspended from his neck, he wears a medal similar to that in the possession of the two sisters. This Indian is Djalma.

His features are at once very noble and very beautiful. His hair of a blue black, parted upon his forehead, falls waving, but not curled over his shoulders; whilst his eyebrows, boldly and yet delicately defined, are of as deep a jet as the long eyelashes, that cast their shadow upon his beardless cheek. His bright, red lips are slightly apart, and he breathes uneasily; his sleep is heavy and troubled, for the heat becomes every moment more and more suffocating.

Without, the silence is profound. Not a breath of air is stirring. Yet now the tall ferns, which cover the soil, begin to move almost imperceptibly, as though their stems were shaken by the slow progress of some crawling body. From time to time, this trifling oscillation suddenly ceases, and all is again motionless. But, after several of these alternations of rustling and deep silence, a human head appears in the midst of the jungle, a little distance from the trunk of the dead tree.

The man to whom it belonged was possessed of a grim countenance, with a complexion the color of greenish bronze, long black hair bound about his temples, eyes brilliant with savage fire, and an expression remarkable for its intelligence and ferocity. Holding his breath, he remained quite still for a moment; then, advancing upon his hands and knees, pushing aside the leaves so gently, that not the slightest noise could be heard, he arrived cautiously and slowly at the trunk of the dead tree, the summit of which nearly touched the roof of the ajoupa.

This man, of Malay origin, belonging to the sect of the Lughardars (Stranglers), after having again listened, rose almost entirely from amongst the brushwood. With the exception of white cotton drawers, fastened around his middle by a parti-colored sash, he was completely naked. His bronze, supple, and nervous limbs were overlaid with a thick coat of oil. Stretching himself along the huge trunk on the side furthest from the cabin, and thus sheltered by the whole breadth of the tree with its surrounding creepers, he began to climb silently, with as much patience as caution. In the undulations of his form, in the flexibility of his movements, in the restrained vigor, which fully put forth would have been alarming, there was some resemblance to the stealthy and treacherous advance of the tiger upon its prey.

Having reached, completely unperceived, the inclined portion of the tree, which almost touched the roof of the cabin, he was only separated from the window by a distance of about a foot. Cautiously advancing his head, he looked down into the interior, to see how he might best find an entrance.

At sight of Djalma in his deep sleep, the Thug's bright eyes glittered with increased brilliancy; a nervous contraction, or rather a mute, ferocious laugh, curling the corners of his mouth, drew them up towards the cheekbones, and exposed rows of teeth, filed sharp like the points of a saw, and dyed of a shining black.

Djalma was lying in such a manner and so near the door of the ajoupa, which opened inwards, that, were it moved in the least, he must be instantly awakened. The Strangler, with his body still sheltered by the tree, wishing to examine more attentively the interior of the cabin, leaned very forward, and in order to maintain his balance, lightly rested his hand on the ledge of the opening that served for a window. This movement shook the large cactus-flowers, within which the little serpent lay curled, and, darting forth it twisted itself rapidly round the wrist of the Strangler. Whether from pain or surprise, the man uttered a low cry; and as he drew back swiftly, still holding by the trunk of the tree, he perceived that Djalma had moved.

The young Indian, though retaining his supine posture, had half opened his eyes, and turned his head towards the window, whilst his breast heaved with a deep-drawn sigh, for, beneath that thick dome of moist verdure, the concentrated heat was intolerable.

Hardly had he moved, when, from behind the tree, was heard the shrill, brief, sonorous note, which the bird of paradise titters when it takes its flight - a cry which resembles that of the pheasant. This note was soon repeated, but more faintly, as though the brilliant bird were already at a distance. Djalma, thinking he had discovered the cause of the noise which had aroused him for an instant, stretched out the arm upon which his head had rested, and went to sleep again, with scarcely any change of position.

For some minutes, the most profound silence once more reigned in this solitude, and everything remained motionless.

The Strangler, by his skillful imitation of the bird, had repaired the imprudence of that exclamation of surprise and pain, which the reptile bite had forced from him. When he thought all was safe, he again advanced his head, and saw the young Indian once more plunged in sleep. Then he descended the tree with the same precautions, though his left hand was somewhat swollen from the sting of the serpent, and disappeared in the jungle.

At that instant a song of monotonous and melancholy cadence

was heard in the distance. The Strangler raised himself, and listened attentively, and his face took an expression of surprise and deadly anger. The song came nearer and nearer to the cabin, and, in a few seconds, an Indian, passing through an open space in the jungle, approached the spot where the Thug lay concealed.

The latter unwound from his waist a long thin cord, to one of the ends of which was attached a leaden ball, of the form and size of an egg; having fastened the other end of this cord to his right wrist, the Strangler again listened, and then disappeared, crawling through the tall grass in the direction of the Indian, who still advanced slowly, without interrupting his soft and plaintive song.

He was a young fellow scarcely twenty, with a bronzed complexion, the slave of Djalma, his vest of blue cotton was confined at the waist by a parti-colored sash; he wore a red turban, and silver rings in his ears and about his wrists. He was bringing a message to his master, who, during the great heat of the day was reposing in the ajoupa, which stood at some distance from the house he inhabited.

Arriving at a place where two paths separated, the slave, without hesitation took that which led to the cabin, from which he was now scarce forty paces distant.

One of those enormous Java butterflies, whose wings extend six or eight inches in length, and offer to the eye two streaks of gold on a ground of ultramarine, fluttering from leaf to leaf, alighted on a bush of Cape jasmine, within the reach of the young Indian. The slave stopped in his song, stood still, advanced first a foot, then a hand, and seized the butterfly.

Suddenly he sees a dark figure rise before him; he hears a whizzing noise like that of a sling; he feels a cord, thrown with as much rapidity as force, encircle his neck with a triple band; and, almost in the same instant, the leaden ball strikes violently against the back of his head.

This attack was so abrupt and unforseen, that Djalma's servant could not even utter a single cry, a single groan. He tottered - the Strangler gave a vigorous pull at the cord - the bronzed countenance of the slave became purple, and he fell upon his knees, convulsively moving his arms. Then the Strangler threw him quite down, and pulled the cord so violently, that the blood spurted from the skin. The victim struggled for a moment - and all was over.

During his short but intense agony, the murderer, kneeling before his victim, and watching with ardent eye his least convulsions, seemed plunged into an ecstasy of ferocious joy. His nostrils dilated, the veins of his neck and temples were swollen, and the same savage laugh, which had curled his lips at the aspect of the sleeping Djalma, again displayed his pointed black teeth, which a nervous trembling of the jaws made to chatter. But soon he crossed his arms upon his heaving breast, bowed his forehead, and murmured some mysterious words, which sounded like an invocation or a prayer. Immediately after, he returned to the contemplation of the dead body. The hyena and the tiger-cat, who, before devouring, crouch beside the prey that they have surprised or hunted down, have not a wilder or more sanguinary look than this man.

But, remembering that his task was not yet accomplished tearing himself unwillingly from the hideous spectacle, he unbound the cord from the neck of his victim, fastened it round his own body, dragged the corpse out of the path, and, without attempting to rob it of its silver rings, concealed it in a thick part of the jungle.

Then the Strangler again began to creep on his knees and belly, till he arrived at the cabin of Djalma - that cabin constructed of mats suspended from bamboos. After listening attentively, he drew from his girdle a knife, the sharp-pointed blade of which was wrapped in a fig-leaf, and made in the matting an incision of three feet in length. This was done with such quickness, and with so fine a blade, that the light touch of the diamond cutting glass would have made more noise. Seeing, by means of this opening, which was to serve him for a passage, that Djalma was still fast asleep, the Thug, with incredible temerity, glided into the cabin.

CHAPTER XVIII

THE TATTOOING

The heavens, which had been till now of transparent blue, became gradually of a greenish tint, and the sun was veiled in red, lurid vapor. This strange light gave to every object a weird appearance, of which one might form an idea, by looking at a landscape through a piece of copper colored glass. In those climates, this phenomenon, when united with an increase of burning heat, always announces the approach of a storm.

From time to time there was a passing odor of sulphur; then the leaves, slightly shaken by electric currents, would tremble upon their stalks; till again all would return to the former motionless silence. The weight of the burning atmosphere, saturated with sharp perfumes, became almost intolerable. Large drops of sweat stood in pearls on the forehead of Djalma, still plunged in enervating sleep - for it no longer resembled rest, but a painful stupor.

The Strangler glided like a reptile along the sides of the ajoupa, and, crawling on his belly, arrived at the sleeping-mat of Djalma, beside which he squatted himself, so as to occupy as little space as possible. Then began a fearful scene, by reason of the mystery and silence which surrounded it.

Djalma's life was at the mercy of the Strangler. The latter, resting upon his hands and knees, with his neck stretched forward, his eye fixed and dilated, continued motionless as a wild beast about to spring. Only a slight nervous trembling of the jaws agitated that mask of bronze.

But soon his hideous features revealed a violent struggle that was passing within him - a struggle between the thirst, the craving for the enjoyment of murder, which the recent assassination of the slave had made still more active, and the orders he had received not to attempt the life of Djalma, though the design, which brought him to the ajoupa, might perhaps be as fatal to the young Indian as death itself. Twice did the Strangler, with look of flame, resting only on his left hand, seize with his right the rope's end; and twice his hand fell - the instinct of murder yielding to a powerful will, of which the Malay acknowledged the irresistible empire.

In him, the homicidal craving must have amounted to madness, for, in these hesitations, he lost much precious time: at any moment, Djalma, whose vigor, skill, and courage were known and feared, might awake from his sleep, and, though unarmed, he would prove a terrible adversary. At length the Thug made up his mind; with a suppressed sigh of regret, he set about accomplishing his task.

This task would have appeared impossible to any one else. The reader may judge.

Djalma, with his face turned towards the left, leaned his head upon his curved arm. It was first necessary, without waking him, to oblige him to turn his face towards the right (that is, towards the door), so that, in case of his being half-roused, his first glance might not fall upon the Strangler. The latter, to accomplish his projects, would have to remain many minutes in the cabin.

The heavens became darker; the heat arrived at its last degree of intensity; everything combined to increase the torpor of the sleeper, and so favor the Strangler's designs. Kneeling down close to Djalma, he began, with the tips of his supple, well-oiled fingers, to stroke the brow, temples, and eyelids of the young Indian, but with such extreme lightness, that the contact of the two skins was hardly sensible. When this kind of magnetic incantation had lasted for some seconds, the sweat, which bathed the forehead of Djalma, became more abundant: he heaved a smothered sigh, and the muscles of his face gave several twitches, for the strokings, although too light to rouse him, yet caused in him a feeling of indefinable uneasiness.

Watching him with his restless and burning eye, the Strangler continued his maneuvers with so much patience, that Djalma, still sleeping, but no longer able to bear this vague, annoying sensation, raised his right hand mechanically to his face, as if he would have brushed away an importunate insect. But he had not strength to do it; almost immediately after, his hand, inert and heavy, fell back upon his chest. The Strangler saw, by this symptom, that he was attaining his object, and continued to stroke, with the same address, the eyelids, brow, and temples.

Whereupon Djalma, more and more oppressed by heavy sleep, and having neither strength nor will to raise his hand to his face, mechanically turned round his head, which fell languidly upon his right shoulder, seeking by this change of attitude, to escape from the disagreeable sensation which pursued him. The first point gained, the Strangler could act more freely.

To render as profound as possible the sleep he had half interrupted, he now strove to imitate the vampire, and, feigning the action of a fan, he rapidly moved his extended hands about the burning face of the young Indian. Alive to a feeling of such sudden and delicious coolness, in the height of suffocating heat, the countenance of Djalma brightened, his bosom heaved, his half-opened lips drank in the grateful air, and he fell into a sleep only the more invincible, because it had been at first disturbed, and was now yielded to under the influence of a pleasing sensation.

A sudden flash of lightning illumined the shady dome that sheltered the ajoupa: fearing that the first clap of thunder might rouse the young Indian, the Strangler hastened to complete his Task. Djalma lay on his back, with his head resting on his right shoulder, and his left arm extended; the Thug, crouching at his left side, ceased by degrees the process of fanning; then, with incredible dexterity, he succeeded in rolling up, above the elbow, the long wide sleeve of white muslin that covered the left arm of the sleeper.

He next drew from the pocket of his drawers a copper box, from which he took a very fine, sharp-pointed needle, and a piece of a black-looking root. He pricked this root several times with the needle, and on each occasion there issued from it a white, glutinous liquid.

When the Strangler thought the needle sufficiently impregnated with this juice, he bent down, and began to blow gently over the inner surface of Djalma's arm, so as to cause a fresh sensation of coolness; then, with the point of his needle, he traced almost imperceptibly on the skin of the sleeping youth some mysterious and symbolical signs. All this was performed so cleverly and the point of the needle was so fine and keen, that Djalma did not feel the action of the acid upon the skin.

The signs, which the Strangler had traced, soon appeared on the surface, at first in characters of a pale rose-color, as fine as a hair; but such was the slowly corrosive power of the juice, that, as it worked and spread beneath the skin, they would become in a few hours of a violet red, and as apparent as they were now almost invisible.

The Strangler, having so perfectly succeeded in his project, threw a last look of ferocious longing on the slumbering Indian, and creeping away from the mat, regained the opening by which he had entered the cabin; next, closely uniting the edges of the incision, so as to obviate all suspicion, he disappeared just as the thunder began to rumble hoarsely in the distance.[4]

[4] We read in the letters of the late Victor Jacquemont upon India, with regard to the incredible dexterity of these men: "They crawl on the ground, ditches, in the furrows of fields, imitate a hundred different voices, and dissipate the effect of any accidental noise by raising the yelp of the jackal or note of some bird - then are silent, and another imitates the call of the same animal in the distance. They can molest a sleeper by all sorts of noises and slight touches, and make his body and limbs take any position which suits their purpose." Count Edward de Warren, in his excellent work on English India, which we shall have again occasion to quote, expresses himself in the same manner as to the inconceivable address of the Indians: "They have the art," says he, "to rob you, without interrupting your sleep, of the very sheet in which you are enveloped. This is not 'a traveller's tale.' but a fact. The movements of the bheel are those of the serpent. If you sleep in your tent, with a servant lying across each entrance, the bheel will come and crouch on the outside, in some shady corner, where he can hear the breathing of those within. As soon as the European sleeps, he feels sure of success, for the Asiatic will not long resist the attraction of repose. At the proper moment, he makes a vertical incision in the cloth of the tent, on the spot where he happens to be, and just large enough to admit him. He glides through like a phantom, without making the least grain of sand creak beneath his tread. He is perfectly naked, and all his body is rubbed over with oil; a two-edged knife is suspended from his neck. He will squat down close to your couch, and, with incredible coolness and dexterity, will gather up the sheet in very little folds, so as to occupy the least surface possible; then, passing to the other side, he will lightly tickle the sleeper, whom he seems to magnetize, till the latter shrinks back involuntarily, and ends by turning round, and leaving the sheet folded behind him. Should he awake, and strive to seize the robber, he catches at a slippery form, which slides through his hands like an eel; should he even succeed in seizing him, it would be fatal - the dagger strikes him to the heart, he falls bathed in his blood, and the assassin disappears." - E. S.

CHAPTER XIX

THE SMUGGLER

The tempest of the morning has long been over. The sun is verging towards the horizon. Some hours have elapsed, since the Strangler introduced himself into Djalma's cabin, and tattooed him with a mysterious sign during his sleep.

A horseman advances rapidly down a long avenue of spreading trees. Sheltered by the thick and verdant arch, a thousand birds salute the splendid evening with songs and circlings; red and green parrots climb, by help of their hooked beaks, to the top of pink-blossomed acacias; large Morea birds of the finest and richest blue, whose throats and long tails change in the light to a golden brown, are chasing the prince oriels, clothed in their glossy feathers of black and orange; Kolo doves, of a changeable violet hue, are gently cooing by the side of the birds of paradise, in whose brilliant plumage are mingled the prismatic colors of the emerald and ruby, the topaz and sapphire.

This avenue, a little raised, commanded a view of a small pond, which reflected at intervals the green shade of tamarind trees. In the calm, limpid waters, many fish were visible, some with silver scales and purple fins, others gleaming with azure and vermilion; so still were they that they looked as if set in a mass of bluish crystal, and, as they dwelt motionless near the surface of the pool, on which played a dazzling ray of the sun, they revelled in the enjoyment of the light and heat. A thousand insects - living gems, with wings of flame - glided, fluttered and buzzed over the transparent wave, in which, at an extraordinary depth, were mirrored the variegated tints of the aquatic plants on the bank.

It is impossible to give an adequate idea of the exuberant nature of this scene, luxuriant in the sunlight, colors, and perfumes, which served, so to speak, as a frame to the young and brilliant rider, who was advancing along the avenue. It was Djalma. He had not yet perceived the indelible marks, which the Strangler had traced upon his left arm.

His Japanese mare, of slender make, full of fire and vigor, is black as night. A narrow red cloth serves instead of saddle. To moderate the impetuous bounds of the animal, Djalma uses a small steel bit, with headstall and reins of twisted scarlet silk, fine as a thread.

Not one of those admirable riders, sculptured so masterly on the frieze of the Parthenon, sits his horse more gracefully and proudly than this young Indian, whose fine face, illumined by the setting sun, is radiant with serene happiness; his eyes sparkle with joy, and his dilated nostrils and unclosed lips inhale with delight the balmy breeze, that brings to him the perfume of flowers and the scent of fresh leaves, for the trees are still moist from the abundant rain that fell after the storm.

A red cap, similar to that worn by the Greeks, surmounting the black locks of Djalma, sets off to advantage the golden tint of his complexion; his throat is bare; he is clad in his robe of white muslin with large sleeves, confined at the waist by a scarlet sash; very full drawers, in white cotton stuff, leave half uncovered his tawny and polished legs; their classic curve stands out from the dark sides of the horse, which he presses tightly between his muscular calves. He has no stirrups; his foot, small and narrow, is shod with a sandal of morocco leather.

The rush of his thoughts, by turns impetuous and restrained, was expressed in some degree by the pace he imparted to his horse - now bold and precipitate, like the flight of unbridled imagination - now calm and measured, like the reflection which succeeds an idle dream. But, in all this fantastic course, his least movements were distinguished by a proud, independent and somewhat savage grace.

Dispossessed of his paternal territory by the English, and at first detained by them as a state-prisoner after the death of his father - who (as M. Joshua Van Dael had written to M. Rodin) had fallen sword in hand - Djalma had at length been restored to liberty. Abandoning the continent of India, and still accompanied by General Simon, who had lingered hard by the prison of his old friend's son, the young Indian came next to Batavia, the birthplace of his mother, to collect the modest inheritance of his maternal ancestors. And amongst this property, so long despised or forgotten by his father, he found some important papers, and a medal exactly similar to that worn by Rose and Blanche.

General Simon was not more surprised than pleased at this discovery, which not only established a tie of kindred between his wife and Djalma's mother, but which also seemed to promise great advantages for the future. Leaving Djalma at Batavia, to terminate some business there, he had gone to the neighboring island of Sumatra, in the hope of finding a vessel that would make the passage to Europe directly and rapidly; for it was now necessary that, cost what it might, the young Indian also should be at Paris on the 13th February, 1832. Should General Simon find a vessel ready to sail for Europe, he was to return immediately, to fetch Djalma; and the latter, expecting him daily, was now going to the pier of Batavia, hoping to see the father of Rose and Blanche arrive by the mail boat from Sumatra.

A few words are here necessary on the early life of the son of Kadja sing.

Having lost his mother very young, and brought up with rude

simplicity, he had accompanied his father, whilst yet a child, to the great tiger hunts, as dangerous as battles; and, in the first dawn of youth, he had followed him to the stern bloody war, which he waged in defence of his country. Thus living, from the time of his mother's death, in the midst of forests and mountains and continual combats, his vigorous and ingenuous nature had preserved itself pure, and he well merited the name of "The Generous" bestowed on him. Born a prince, he was - which by no means follows - a prince indeed. During the period of his captivity, the silent dignity of his bearing had overawed his jailers. Never a reproach, never a complaint - a proud and melancholy calm was all that he opposed to a treatment as unjust as it was barbarous, until he was restored to freedom.

Having thus been always accustomed to a patriarchal life, or to a war of mountaineers, which he had only quitted to pass a few months in prison, Djalma knew nothing, so to speak, of civilized society. Without its exactly amounting to a defect, he certainly carried his good qualities to their extreme limits. Obstinately faithful to his pledged word, devoted to the death, confiding to blindness, good almost to a complete forgetfulness of himself, he was inflexible towards ingratitude, falsehood, or perfidy. He would have felt no compunction to sacrifice a traitor, because, could he himself have committed a treason, he would have thought it only just to expiate it with his life.

He was, in a word, the man of natural feelings, absolute and entire. Such a man, brought into contact with the temperaments, calculations, falsehoods, deceptions, tricks, restrictions, and hollowness of a refined society, such as Paris, for example, would, without doubt, form a very curious subject for speculation. We raise this hypothesis, because, since his journey to France had been determined on, Djalma had one fixed, ardent desire - to be in Paris.

In Paris - that enchanted city - of which, even in Asia, the land of enchantment, so many marvelous tales were told.

What chiefly inflamed the fresh, vivid imagination of the young Indian, was the thought of French women - those attractive Parisian beauties, miracles of elegance and grace, who eclipsed, he was informed, even the magnificence of the capitals of the civilized world. And at this very moment, in the brightness of that warm and splendid evening, surrounded by the intoxication of flowers and perfumes, which accelerated the pulses of his young fiery heart, Djalma was dreaming of those exquisite creatures, whom his fancy loved to clothe in the most ideal garbs.

It seemed to him as if, at the end of the avenue, in the midst of that sheet of golden light, which the trees encompassed with their full, green arch, he could see pass and repass, white and sylph-like, a host of adorable and voluptuous phantoms, that threw him kisses from the tips of their rosy fingers. Unable to restrain his burning emotions, carried away by a strange enthusiasm, Djalma uttered exclamations of joy, deep, manly, and sonorous, and made his vigorous courser bound under him in the excitement of a mad delight. Just then a sunbeam, piercing the dark vault of the avenue, shone full upon him.

For several minutes, a man had been advancing rapidly along a path, which, at its termination, intersected the avenue diagonally. He stopped a moment in the shade, looking at Djalma with astonishment. It was indeed a charming sight, to behold, in the midst of a blaze of dazzling lustre, this youth, so handsome, joyous, and ardent, clad in his white and flowing vestments, gayly and lightly seated on his proud black mare, who covered her red bridle with her foam, and whose long tail and thick mane floated on the evening breeze.

But, with that reaction which takes place in all human desires, Djalma soon felt stealing over him a sentiment of soft, undefinable melancholy. He raised his hand to his eyes, now dimmed with moisture, and allowed the reins to fall on the mane of his docile steed, which, instantly stopping, stretched out its long neck, and turned its head in the direction of the personage, whom it could see approaching through the coppice.

This man, Mahal the Smuggler, was dressed nearly like European sailors. He wore jacket and trousers of white duck, a broad red sash, and a very low-crowned straw hat. His face was brown, with strongly-marked features, and, though forty years of age, he was quite beardless.

In another moment, Mahal was close to the young Indian. "You are Prince Djalma?" said he, in not very good French, raising his hand respectfully to his hat.

"What would you?" said the Indian.

"You are the son of Kadja-sing?"

"Once again, what would you?"

"The friend of General Simon?"

"General Simon?" cried Djalma.

"You are going to meet him, as you have gone every evening, since you expect his return from Sumatra?"

"Yes, but how do you know all this?" said the Indian looking at the Smuggler with as much surprise as curiosity.

"Is he not to land at Batavia, to-day or to-morrow?"

"Are you sent by him?"

"Perhaps," said Mahal, with a distrustful air. "But are you really the son of Kadja-sing?"

"Yes, I tell you - but where have you seen General Simon?"

"If you are the son of Kadja-sing," resumed Mahal, continuing to regard Djalma with a suspicious eye, "what is your surname?"

"My sire was called the 'Father of the Generous,'" answered the young Indian, as a shade of sorrow passed over his fine countenance.

These words appeared in part to convince Mahal of the identity of Djalma; but, wishing doubtless to be still more certain, he resumed: "You must have received, two days ago, a letter from General Simon, written from Sumatra?"

"Yes; but why so many questions?"

"To assure myself that you are really the son of Kadja-sing, and to execute the orders I have received."

"From whom?"

"From General Simon."

"But where is he?"

"When I have proof that you are Prince Djalma, I will tell you. I was informed that you would be mounted on a black mare, with a red bridle. But -"

"By the soul of my mother! speak what you have to say!"

"I will tell you all - if you can tell me what was the printed paper, contained in the last letter that General Simon wrote you from Sumatra."

"It was a cutting from a French newspaper."

"Did it announce good or bad news for the general?"

"Good news - for it related that, during his absence, they had acknowledged the last rank and title bestowed on him by the Emperor, as they had done for others of his brothers in arms, exiled like him."

"You are indeed Prince Djalma," said the Smuggler, after a moment's reflection. "I may speak. General Simon landed last night in Java, but on a desert part of the coast."

"On a desert part?"

"Because he has to hide himself."

"Hide himself!" exclaimed Djalma, in amazement; "why?"

"That I don't know."

"But where is he?" asked Djalma, growing pale with alarm.

"He is three leagues hence - near the sea-shore - in the ruins of Tchandi."

"Obliged to hide himself!" repeated Djalma, and his countenance expressed increasing surprise and anxiety.

"Without being certain, I think it is because of a duel he fought in Sumatra," said the Smuggler, mysteriously.

"A duel - with whom?"

"I don't know - I am not at all certain on the subject. But do you know the ruins of Tchandi?"

"Yes."

"The general expects you there; that is what he ordered me to tell you."

"So you came with him from Sumatra?"

"I was pilot of the little smuggling coaster, that landed him in the night on a lonely beach. He knew that you went every day to the mole, to wait for him; I was almost sure that I should meet you. He gave me details about the letter you received from him as a proof that he had sent me. If he could have found the means of writing, he would have written."

"But he did not tell you why he was obliged to hide himself?"

"He told me nothing. Certain words made me suspect what I told you - a duel."

Knowing the mettle of General Simon, Djalma thought the suspicions of the Smuggler not unfounded. After a moment's silence he said to him: "Can you undertake to lead home my horse? My dwelling is without the town - there, in the midst of those trees - by the side of the new mosque. In ascending the mountain of Tchandi, my horse would be in my way; I shall go much faster on foot."

"I know where you live; General Simon told me. I should have gone there if I had not met you. Give me your horse."

Djalma sprang lightly to the ground, threw the bridle to Mahal, unrolled one end of his sash, took out a silk purse, and gave it to the Smuggler, saying: "You have been faithful and obedient. Here! - it is a trifle - but I have no more."

"Kadja-sing was rightly called the 'Father of the Generous,'" said the Smuggler, bowing with respect and gratitude. He took the road to Batavia, leading Djalma's horse. The young Indian, on the contrary, plunged into the coppice, and, walking with great strides, he directed his course towards the mountain, on which were the ruins of Tchandi, where he could not arrive before night.

CHAPTER XX

M. JOSHUA VAN DAEL

M. Joshua Van Dael a Dutch merchant, and correspondent of M. Rodin, was born at Batavia, the capital of the island of Java; his parents had sent him to be educated at Pondicherry, in a celebrated religious house, long established in that place, and belonging to the "Society of Jesus." It was there that he was initiated into the order as "professor of the three vows," or lay member, commonly called "temporal coadjutor."

Joshua was a man of probity that passed for stainless; of strict accuracy in business, cold, careful, reserved, and remarkably skillful and sagacious; his financial operations were almost always successful, for a protecting power gave him ever in time, knowledge of events which might advantageously influence his commercial transactions. The religious house of Pondicherry was interested in his affairs, having charged him with the exportation and exchange of the produce of its large possessions in this colony.

Speaking little, hearing much, never disputing, polite in the extreme - giving seldom, but with choice and purpose - Joshua, without inspiring sympathy, commanded generally that cold respect, which is always paid to the rigid moralist; for instead of yielding to the influence of lax and dissolute colonial manners, he appeared to live with great regularity, and his exterior had something of austerity about it, which tended to overawe.

The following scene took place at Batavia, while Djalma was on his way to the ruins of Tchandi in the hope of meeting General Simon.

M. Joshua had just retired into his cabinet, in which were many shelves filled with paper boxes, and huge ledgers and cash boxes lying open upon desks. The only window of this apartment, which was on the ground floor, looked out upon a narrow empty court, and was protected externally by strong iron bars; instead of glass, it was fitted with a Venetian blind, because of the extreme heat of the climate.

M. Joshua, having placed upon his desk a taper in a glass globe, looked at the clock. "Half-past nine," said he. "Mahal ought soon to be here."

Saying this, he went out, passing through an antechamber, opened a second thick door, studded with nail-heads, in the Dutch fashion, cautiously entered the court (so as not to be heard by the people in the house), and drew back the secret bolt of a gate six feet high, formidably garnished with iron spikes. Leaving this gate unfastened, he regained his cabinet, after he had successively and carefully closed the two other doors behind him.

M. Joshua next seated himself at his desk, and took from a drawer a long letter, or rather statement, commenced some time before, and continued day by day. It is superfluous to observe, that the letter already mentioned, as addressed to M. Rodin, was anterior to the liberation of Djalma and his arrival at Batavia.

The present statement was also addressed to M. Rodin, and Van Dael thus went on with it:

"Fearing the return of General Simon, of which I had been informed by intercepting his letters - I have already told you, that I had succeeded in being employed by him as his agent here; having then read his letters, and sent them on as if untouched to Djalma, I felt myself obliged, from the pressure of the circumstances, to have recourse to extreme measures - taking care always to preserve appearances, and rendering at the same time a signal service to humanity, which last reason chiefly decided me.

"A new danger imperiously commanded these measures. The steamship 'Ruyter' came in yesterday, and sails tomorrow in the course of the day. She is to make the voyage to Europe via the Arabian Gulf; her passengers will disembark at Suez, cross the Isthmus, and go on board another vessel at Alexandria, which will bring them to France. This voyage, as rapid as it is direct, will not take more than seven or eight weeks. We are now at the end of October; Prince Djalma might then be in France by the commencement of the month of January; and according to your instructions, of which I know not the motive, but which I execute with zeal and submission, his departure must be prevented at all hazards, because, you tell me, some of the gravest interests of the Society would be compromised, by the arrival of this young Indian in Paris before the 13th of February. Now, if I succeed, as I hope, in making him miss this opportunity of the 'Ruyter' it will be materially impossible for him to arrive in France before the month of April; for the 'Ruyter' is the only vessel which makes the direct passage, the others taking at least four or five months to reach Europe.

"Before telling you the means which I have thought right to employ, to detain Prince Djalma - of the success of which means I am yet uncertain - it is well that you should be acquainted with the following facts.

"They have just discovered, in British India, a community whose members call themselves 'Brothers of the Good Work,' or 'Phansegars,' which signifies simply 'Thugs' or 'Stranglers;' these murderers do not shed blood, but strangle their victims, less for the purpose of robbing them, than in obedience to a homicidal vocation, and to the laws of an infernal divinity named by them 'Bowanee.'

"I cannot better give you an idea of this horrible sect, than by transcribing here some lines from the introduction of a report by Colonel Sleeman, who has hunted out this dark association with indefatigable zeal. The report in question was published about two months ago. Here is the extract; it is the colonel who speaks:

"'From 1822 to 1824, when I was charged with the magistracy and civil administration of the district of Nersingpore, not a murder, not the least robbery was committed by an ordinary criminal, without my being immediately informed of it; but if any one had come and told me at this period, that a band of hereditary assassins by profession lived in the village of Kundelie, within about four hundred yards of my court of justice - that the beautiful groves of the village of Mundesoor, within a day's march of my residence, formed one of the most frightful marts of assassination in all India - that numerous bands of 'Brothers of the Good Work,' coming from Hindostan and the Deccan, met annually beneath these shades, as at a solemn festival, to exercise their dreadful vocation upon all the roads which cross each other in this locality - I should have taken such a person for a madman, or one who had been imposed upon by idle tales. And yet nothing could be truer; hundreds of travellers had been buried every year in the groves of Mundesoor; a whole tribe of assassins lived close to my door, at the very time I was supreme magistrate of the province, and extended their devastations to the cities of Poonah and Hyderabad. I shall never forget, when, to convince me of the fact, one of the chiefs of the Stranglers, who had turned informer against them, caused thirteen bodies to be dug up from the ground beneath my tent, and offered to produce any number from the soil in the immediate vicinity.'[5]

"These few words of Colonel Sleeman will give some idea of this dread society, which has its laws, duties, customs, opposed to all other laws, human and divine. Devoted to each other, even to heroism, blindly obedient to their chiefs, who profess themselves the immediate representatives of their dark divinity, regarding as enemies all who do not belong to them, gaining recruits everywhere by a frightful system of proselytising - these apostles of a religion of murder go preaching their abominable doctrines in the shade, and spreading their immense net over the whole of India.

"Three of their principal chiefs, and one of their adepts, flying from the determined pursuit of the English governor-general, having succeeded in making their escape, had arrived at the Straits of Malacca, at no great distance from our island; a smuggler, who is also something of a pirate, attached to their association, and by name Mahal, took them on board his coasting vessel, and brought them hither, where they think themselves for some time in safety - as, following the advice of the smuggler, they lie concealed in a thick forest, in which are many ruined temples and numerous subterranean retreats.

"Amongst these chiefs, all three remarkably intelligent, there is one in particular, named Faringhea, whose extraordinary energy and eminent qualities make him every way redoubtable. He is of the mixed race, half white and Hindoo, has long inhabited towns in which are European factories and speaks English and French very well. The other two chiefs are a Negro and a Hindoo; the adept is a Malay.

"The smuggler, Mahal, considering that he could obtain a large reward by giving up these three chiefs and their adept, came to me, knowing, as all the world knows, my intimate relations with a person who has great influence with our governor. Two days ago, he offered me, on certain conditions, to deliver up the Negro, the half-caste, the Hindoo, and the Malay. These conditions are - a considerable sum of money, and a free passage on board a vessel sailing for Europe or America, in order to escape the implacable vengeance of the Thugs.

"I joyfully seized the occasion to hand over three such murderers to human justice, and I promised Mahal to arrange matters for him with the governor, but also on certain conditions, innocent in themselves, and which concerned Djalma. Should my project succeed, I will explain myself more at length; I shall soon know the result, for I expect Mahal every minute.

"But before I close these despatches, which are to go tomorrow by the 'Ruyter' - in which vessel I have also engaged a passage for Mahal the Smuggler, in the event of the success of my plans - I must include in parentheses a subject of some importance.

"In my last letter, in which I announced to you the death of Djalma's father, and his own imprisonment by the English, I asked for some information as to the solvency of Baron Tripeaud, banker and manufacturer at Paris, who has also an agency at Calcutta. This information will now be useless, if what I have just learned should, unfortunately, turn out to be correct, and it will be for you to act according to circumstances.

"This house at Calcutta owes considerable sums both to me and our colleague at Pondicherry, and it is said that M. Tripeaud has involved himself to a dangerous extent in attempting to ruin, by opposition, a very flourishing establishment, founded some time ago by M. Francois Hardy, an eminent manufacturer. I am assured that M. Tripeaud has already sunk and lost a large capital in this enterprise: he has no doubt done a great deal of harm to M. Francois Hardy; but he has also, they say, seriously compromised his own fortune - and, were he to fail, the effects of his disaster would be very fatal to us, seeing that he owes a large sum of money to me and to us.

"In this state of things it would be very desirable if, by the employment of the powerful means of every kind at our disposal, we could completely discredit and break down the house of M. Francois Hardy, already shaken by M. Tripeaud's violent opposition. In that case, the latter would soon regain all he has lost; the ruin of his rival would insure his prosperity, and our demands would be securely covered.

"Doubtless, it is painful, it is sad, to be obliged to have recourse to these extreme measures, only to get back our own; but, in these days, are we not surely justified in sometimes using the arms that are incessantly turned against us? If we are reduced to such steps by the injustice and wickedness of men, we may console ourselves with the reflection that we only seek to preserve our worldly possessions, in order to devote them to the greater glory of God; whilst, in the hands of our enemies, those very goods are the dangerous instruments of perdition and scandal.

"After all it is merely a humble proposition that I submit to you. Were it in my power to take an active part in the matter, I should do nothing of myself. My will is not my own. It belongs, with all I possess, to those whom I have sworn absolute obedience."

Here a slight noise interrupted M. Joshua, and drew his attention from his work. He rose abruptly, and went straight to the window. Three gentle taps were given on the outside of one of the slats of the blind.

"Is it you, Mahal?" asked M. Joshua, in a low voice.

"It is I," was answered from without, also in a low tone.

"And the Malay?"

"He has succeeded."

"Really!" cried M. Joshua, with an expression of great satisfaction; "are you sure of it?"

"Quite sure: there is no devil more clever and intrepid."

"And Djalma?"

"The parts of the letter, which I quoted, convinced him that I came from General Simon, and that he would find him at the ruins of Tchandi."

"Therefore, at this moment -"

"Djalma goes to the ruins, where he will encounter the black, the half blood, and the Indian. It is there they have appointed to meet the Malay, who tattooed the prince during his sleep."

"Have you been to examine the subterraneous passage?"

"I went there yesterday. One of the stones of the pedestal of the statue turns upon itself; the stairs are large; it will do."

"And the three chiefs have no suspicion?"

"None - I saw them in the morning - and this evening the Malay came to tell me all, before he went to join them at the ruins of Tchandi - for he had remained hidden amongst the bushes, not daring to go there in the daytime."

"Mahal - if you have told the truth, and if all succeed - your pardon and ample reward are assured to you. Your berth has been taken on board the 'Ruyter;' you will sail to-morrow; you will thus be safe from the malice of the Stranglers, who would follow you hither to revenge the death of their chiefs, Providence having chosen you to deliver those three great criminals to justice. Heaven will bless you! - Go and wait for me at the door of the governor's house; I will introduce you. The matter is so important that I do not hesitate to disturb him thus late in the night. Go quickly! - I will follow on my side."

The steps of Mahal were distinctly audible, as he withdrew precipitately, and then silence reigned once more in the house. Joshua returned to his desk, and hastily added these words to the despatch, which he had before commenced:

"Whatever may now happen, it will be impossible for Djalma to leave Batavia at present. You may rest quite satisfied; he will not be at Paris by the 13th of next February. As I foresaw, I shall have to be up all night. - I am just going to the governor's. To-morrow I will add a few lines to this long statement, which the steamship 'Ruyter' will convey to Europe."

Having locked up his papers, Joshua rang the bell loudly, and, to the great astonishment of his servants, not accustomed to see him leave home in the middle of the night, went in all haste to the residence of the governor of the island.

We now conduct the reader to the ruins of Tchandi.

[5] This report is extracted from Count Edward de Warren's excellent work, "British India in 1831." - E. S.

CHAPTER XXI

THE RUINS OF TCHANDI

To the storm in the middle of the day, the approach of which so well served the Strangler's designs upon Djalma, has succeeded a calm and serene night. The disk of the moon rises slowly behind a mass of lofty ruins, situated on a hill, in the midst of a thick wood, about three leagues from Batavia.

Long ranges of stone, high walls of brick, fretted away by time, porticoes covered with parasitical vegetation, stand out boldly from the sheet of silver light which blends the horizon with the limpid blue of the heavens. Some rays of the moon, gliding through the opening on one of these porticoes, fall upon two colossal statues at the foot of an immense staircase, the loose stones of which are almost entirely concealed by grass, moss, and brambles.

The fragments of one of these statues, broken in the middle, lie strewed upon the ground; the other, which remains whole and standing, is frightful to behold. It represents a man of gigantic proportions, with a head three feet high; the expression of the countenance is ferocious, eyes of brilliant slaty black are set beneath gray brows, the large, deep mouth gapes immoderately, and reptiles have made their nest between the lips of stone; by the light of the moon, a hideous swarm is there dimly visible. A broad girdle, adorned with symbolic ornaments, encircles the body of this statue, and fastens a long sword to its right side. The giant has four extended arms, and, in his great hands, he bears an elephant's head, a twisted serpent, a human skull, and a bird resembling a heron. The moon, shedding her light on the profile of this statue, serves to augment the weirdness of its aspect.

Here and there, enclosed in the half-crumbling walls of brick, are fragments of stone bas-reliefs, very boldly cut; one of those in the best preservation represents a man with the head of an elephant, and the wings of a bat, devouring a child. Nothing can be more gloomy than these ruins, buried among thick trees of a dark green, covered with frightful emblems, and seen by the moonlight, in the midst of the deep silence of night.

Against one of the walls of this ancient temple, dedicated to some mysterious and bloody Javanese divinity, leans a kind of hut, rudely constructed of fragments of brick and stone; the door, made of woven rushes, is open, and a red light streams from it, which throws its rays on the tall grass that covers the ground. Three men are assembled in this hovel, around a clay-lamp, with a wick of cocoanut fibre steeped in palm-oil.

The first of these three, about forty years of age, is poorly clad in the European fashion; his pale, almost white, complexion, announces that he belongs to the mixed race, being offspring of a white father and Indian mother.

The second is a robust African negro, with thick lips, vigorous shoulders, and lank legs; his woolly hair is beginning to turn gray; he is covered with rags, and stands close beside the Indian. The third personage is asleep, and stretched on a mat in the corner of the hovel.

These three men are the three Thuggee chiefs, who, obliged to fly from the continent of India, have taken refuge in Java, under the guidance of Mahal the Smuggler.

"The Malay does not return," said the half-blood, named Faringhea, the most redoubtable chief of this homicidal sect: "in executing our orders, he has perhaps been killed by Djalma."

"The storm of this morning brought every reptile out of the earth," said the negro; "the Malay must have been bitten, and his body ere now a nest of serpents."

"To serve the good work," proceeded Faringhea, with a gloomy air, "one must know how to brave death."

"And to inflict it," added the negro.

A stifled cry, followed by some inarticulate words, here drew the attention of these two men, who hastily turned their heads in the direction of the sleeper. This latter was thirty years old at most. His beardless face, of a bright copper color, his robe of coarse stuff, his turban striped brown and yellow, showed that he belonged to the pure Hindoo race. His sleep appeared agitated by some painful vision; an abundant sweat streamed over his countenance, contracted by terror; he spoke in his dream, but his words were brief and broken, and accompanied with convulsive starts.

"Again that dream!" said Faringhea to the negro. "Always the remembrance of that man."

"What man?"

"Do you not remember, how, five years ago, that savage, Colonel Kennedy, butcher of the Indians, came to the banks of the Ganges, to hunt the tiger, with twenty horses, four elephants, and fifty servants?"

"Yes, yes," said the negro; "and we three, hunters of men, made a better day's sport than he did. Kennedy, his horses, his elephants, and his numerous servants did not get their tiger - but we got ours," he added, with grim irony. "Yes; Kennedy, that tiger with a human face, fell into our ambush, and the brothers of the good work offered up their fine prey to our goddess Bowanee."

"If you remember, it was just at the moment when we gave the last tug to the cord round Kennedy's neck, that we perceived on a sudden a traveller close at hand. He had seen us, and it was necessary to make away with him. Now, since that time," added Faringhea, "the remembrance of the murder of that man pursues our brother in his dreams," and he pointed to the sleeping Indian.

"And even when he is awake," said the negro, looking at Faringhea with a significant air.

"Listen!" said the other, again pointing to the Indian, who, in the agitation of his dream, recommenced talking in abrupt sentences; "listen! he is repeating the answers of the traveller, when we told him he must die, or serve with us on Thuggee. His mind is still impressed - deeply impressed - with those words."

And, in fact, the Indian repeated aloud in his sleep, a sort of mysterious dialogue, of which he himself supplied both questions and answers.

"'Traveller,' said he, in a voice broken by sudden pauses, 'why that black mark on your forehead, stretching from one temple to the other? It is a mark of doom and your look is sad as death. Have you been a victim? Come with us; Kallee will avenge you. You have suffered?' - 'Yes, I have greatly suffered.' - 'For a long time?' - 'Yes, for a very long time.' - 'You suffer even now?' - 'Yes, even now.' - What do you reserve for those who injure you?' - 'My pity.' - 'Will you not render blow for blow?' - 'I will return love for hate.' - 'Who are you, then, that render good for evil?' - 'I am one who loves, and suffers, and forgives.'"

"Brother, do you hear?" said the negro to Faringhea; "he has not forgotten the words of the traveller before his death."

"The vision follows him. Listen! he will speak again. How pale he is!" Still under the influence of his dream, the

Indian continued:

"'Traveller, we are three; we are brave; we have your life in our hands - you have seen us sacrifice to the good work. Be one of us, or die - die - die! Oh, that look! Not thus - do not look at me thus!'" As he uttered these last words, the Indian made a sudden movement, as if to keep off some approaching object, and awoke with a start. Then, passing his hand over his moist forehead, he looked round him with a bewildered eye.

"What! again this dream, brother?" said Faringhea. "For a bold hunter of men, you have a weak head. Luckily, you have a strong heart and arm."

The other remained a moment silent, his face buried in his hands; then he replied: "It is long since I last dreamed of that traveller."

"Is he not dead?" said Faringhea, shrugging his shoulders. "Did you not yourself throw the cord around his neck?"

"Yes," replied the Indian shuddering.

"Did we not dig his grave by the side of Colonel Kennedy's? Did we not bury him with the English butcher, under the sand and the rushes?" said the negro.

"Yes, we dug his grave," said the Indian, trembling; "and yet, only a year ago, I was seated one evening at the gate of Bombay, waiting for one of our brothers - the sun was setting behind the pagoda, to the right of the little hill - the scene is all before me now - I was seated under a figtree - when I heard a slow, firm, even step, and, as I turned round my head - I saw him - coming out of the town."

"A vision," said the negro; "always the same vision!"

"A vision," added Faringhea, "or a vague resemblance."

"I knew him by the black mark on his forehead; it was none but he. I remained motionless with fear, gazing at him with eyes aghast. He stopped, bending upon me his calm, sad look. In spite of myself, I could not help exclaiming: 'It is he!' - 'Yes,' he replied, in his gentle voice, 'it is I. Since all whom thou killest must needs live again,' and he pointed to heaven as he spoke, 'why shouldst thou kill? - Hear me! I have just come from Java; I am going to the other end of the world, to a country of never-melting snow; but, here or there, on plains of fire or plains of ice, I shall still be the same. Even so is it with the souls of those who fall beneath thy kalleepra; in this world or up above, in this garb or in another, the soul must still be a soul; thou canst not smite it. Why then kill?' - and shaking his head sorrowfully, he went on his way, walking slowly, with downcast eyes; he ascended the hill of the pagoda; I watched him as he went, without being able to move: at the moment the sun set, he was standing on the summit of the hill, his tall figure thrown out against the sky - and so he disappeared. Oh! it was he!" added the Indian with a shudder, after a long pause: "it was none but he."

In this story the Indian had never varied, though he had often entertained his companions with the same mysterious adventure. This persistency on his part had the effect of shaking their incredulity, or at least of inducing them to seek some natural cause for this apparently superhuman event.

"Perhaps," said Faringhea, after a moment's reflection, "the knot round the traveller's neck got jammed, and some breath was left him, the air may have penetrated the rushes with which we covered his grave, and so life have returned to him."

"No, no," said the Indian, shaking his head, "this man is not of our race."

"Explain."

"Now I know it!"

"What do you know?"

"Listen!" said the Indian, in a solemn voice; "the number of victims that the children of Bowanee have sacrificed since the commencement of ages, is nothing compared to the immense heap of dead and dying, whom this terrible traveller leaves behind him in his murderous march."

"He?" cried the negro and Faringhea.

"Yes, he!" repeated the Hindoo, with a convinced accent, that made its impression upon his companions. "Hear me and tremble! - When I met this traveller at the gates of Bombay, he came from Java, and was going towards the north, he said. The very next day, the town was a prey to the cholera, and we learned sometime after, that this plague had first broken out here, in Java."

"That is true," said the negro.

"Hear me still further!" resumed the other. "'I am going towards the north, to a country of eternal snow,' said the traveller to me. The cholera also went towards the north, passing through Muscat - Ispahan - Tauris - Tiflis - till it overwhelmed Siberia."

"True," said Faringhea, becoming thoughtful:

"And the cholera," resumed the Indian, "only travelled its five or six leagues a day - a man's tramp - never appeared in two places at once - but swept on slowly, steadily, - even as a man proceeds."

At the mention of this strange coincidence, the Hindoo's companions looked at each other in amazement. After a silence of some minutes, the awe-struck negro said to the last speaker: "So you think that this man -"

"I think that this man, whom we killed, restored to life by

some infernal divinity, has been commissioned to bear this terrible scourge over the earth, and to scatter round his steps that death, from which he is himself secure. Remember!" added the Indian, with gloomy enthusiasm, "this awful wayfarer passed through Java - the cholera wasted Java. He passed through Bombay - the cholera wasted Bombay. He went towards the north - the cholera wasted the north."

So saying, the Indian fell into a profound reverie. The negro and Faringhea were seized with gloomy astonishment.

The Indian spoke the truth as to the mysterious march (still unexplained) of that fearful malady, which has never been known to travel more than five or six leagues a day, or to appear simultaneously in two spots. Nothing can be more curious, than to trace out, on the maps prepared at the period in question, the slow, progressive course of this travelling pestilence, which offers to the astonished eye all the capricious incidents of a tourist's journey. Passing this way rather than that - selecting provinces in a country - towns in a province - one quarter in a town - one street in a quarter - one house in a street - having its place of residence and repose, and then continuing its slow, mysterious, fear inspiring march.

The words of the Hindoo, by drawing attention to these dreadful eccentricities, made a strong impression upon the minds of the negro and Faringhea - wild natures, brought by horrible doctrines to the monomania of murder.

Yes - for this also is an established fact - there have been in India members of an abominable community, who killed without motive, without passion - killed for the sake of killing - for the pleasure of murder - to substitute death for life - to make of a living man a corpse, as they have themselves declared in one of their examinations.

The mind loses itself in the attempt to penetrate the causes of these monstrous phenomena. By what incredible series of events, have men been induced to devote themselves to this priesthood of destruction? Without doubt, such a religion could only flourish in countries given up, like India, to the most atrocious slavery, and to the most merciless iniquity of man to man.

Such a creed! - is it not the hate of exasperated humanity, wound up to its highest pitch by oppression? - May not this homicidal sect, whose origin is lost in the night of ages, have been perpetuated in these regions, as the only possible protest of slavery against despotism? May not an inscrutable wisdom have here made Phansegars, even as are made tigers and serpents?

What is most remarkable in this awful sect, is the mysterious bond, which, uniting its members amongst themselves, separates them from all other men. They have laws and customs of their own, they support and help each other, but for them there is neither country nor family; they owe no allegiance save to a dark, invisible power, whose decrees they obey with blind submission, and in whose name they spread themselves abroad, to make corpses, according to their own savage expression.[6]

For some moments the three Stranglers had maintained a profound silence.

Outside the hut, the moon continued to throw great masses of white radiance, and tall bluish shadows, over the imposing fabric of the ruins; the stars sparkled in the heavens; from time to time, a faint breeze rustled through the thick and varnished leaves of the bananas and the palms.

The pedestal of the gigantic statue, which, still entire, stood on the left side of the portico, rested upon large flagstones, half hidden with brambles. Suddenly, one of these stones appeared to fall in; and from the aperture, which thus formed itself without noise, a man, dressed in uniform, half protruded his body, looked carefully around him, and listened.

Seeing the rays of the lamp, which lighted the interior of the hovel, tremble upon the tall grass, he turned round to make a signal, and soon, accompanied by two other soldiers, he ascended, with the greatest silence and precaution, the last steps of the subterranean staircase, and went gliding amongst the ruins. For a few moments, their moving shadows were thrown upon the moonlit ground; then they disappeared behind some fragments of broken wall.

At the instant when the large stone resumed its place and level, the heads of many other soldiers might have been seen lying close in the excavation. The half-caste, the Indian, and the negro, still seated thoughtfully in the hut, did not perceive what was passing.

[6] The following are some passages from the Count de Warren's very curious book, "British India in 1831:" "Besides the robbers, who kill for the sake of the booty they hope to find upon travellers, there is a class of assassins, forming an organized society, with chiefs of their own, a slang-language, a science, a free-masonry, and even a religion, which has its fanaticism and its devotion, its agents, emissaries, allies, its militant forces, and its passive adherents, who contribute their money to the good work. This is the community of the Thugs or Phansegars (deceivers or stranglers, from thugna, to deceive, and phansna, to strangle), a religious and economical society, which speculates with the human race by exterminating men; its origin is lost in the night of ages.

"Until 1810 their existence was unknown, not only to the European conquerors, but even to the native governments. Between the years 1816 and 1830, several of their bands were taken in the act, and punished: but until this last epoch, all the revelations made on the subject by officers of great experience, had appeared too monstrous to obtain the attention or belief of the public; they had been rejected and despised as the dreams of a heated imagination. And yet for many years, at the very least for half a century, this social wound had been frightfully on the increase, devouring the population from the

Himalayas to Cape Comorin and from Cutch to Assam.

"It was in the year 1830 that the revelations of a celebrated chief, whose life was spared on condition of his denouncing his accomplices, laid bare the whole system. The basis of the Thuggee Society is a religious belief - the worship of Bowanee, a gloomy divinity, who is only pleased with carnage, and detests above all things the human race. Her most agreeable sacrifices are human victims, and the more of these her disciple may have offered up in this world the more he will be recompensed in the next by all the delights of soul and sense, by women always beautiful, and joys eternally renewed. If the assassin meets the scaffold in his career, he dies with the enthusiasm of a martyr, because he expects his reward. To obey his divine mistress, he murders, without anger and without remorse, the old man, woman and child; whilst, to his fellow-religionists, he may be charitable, humane, generous, devoted, and may share all in common with them, because, like himself, they are the ministers and adopted children of Bowanee. The destruction of his fellow-creatures, not belonging to his community - the diminution of the human race - that is the primary object of his pursuit; it is not as a means of gain, for though plunder may be a frequent, and doubtless an agreeable accessory, it is only secondary in his estimation. Destruction is his end, his celestial mission, his calling; it is also a delicious passion, the most captivating of all sports - this hunting of men! - 'You find great pleasure,' said one of those that were condemned, 'in tracking the wild beast to his den, in attacking the boar, the tiger, because there is danger to brave, energy and courage to display. Think how this attraction must be redoubled, when the contest is with man, when it is man that is to be destroyed. Instead of the single faculty of courage, all must be called into action - courage, cunning, foresight, eloquence, intrigue. What springs to put in motion! what plans to develop! To sport with all the passions, to touch the chords of love and friendship, and so draw the prey into one's net - that is a glorious chase - it is a delight, a rapture, I tell you!'

"Whoever was in India in the years 1831 and 1832, must remember the stupor and affright, which the discovery of this vast infernal machine spread through all classes of society. A great number of magistrates and administrators of provinces refused to believe in it, and could not be brought to comprehend that such a system had so long preyed on the body politic, under their eyes as it were, silently, and without betraying itself." - See "British India in 183," by Count Edward de Warren, 2 vols. in 8vo. Paris, 1844. - E. S.

CHAPTER XXII

THE AMBUSCADE

The half-blood Faringhea, wishing doubtless to escape from the dark thoughts which the words of the Indian on the mysterious course of the Cholera had raised within him, abruptly changed the subject of conversation. His eye shone with lurid fire, and his countenance took an expression of savage enthusiasm, as he cried: "Bowanee will always watch over us, intrepid hunters of men! Courage, brothers, courage! The world is large; our prey is everywhere. The English may force us to quit India, three chiefs of the good work - but what matter? We leave there our brethren, secret, numerous, and terrible, as black scorpions, whose presence is only known by their mortal sting. Exiles will widen our domains. Brother, you shall have America!" said he to the Hindoo, with an inspired air. "Brother, you shall have Africa!" said he to the negro. "Brothers, I will take Europe! Wherever men are to be found, there must be oppressors and victims - wherever there are victims, there must be hearts swollen with hate - it is for us to inflame that hate with all the ardor of vengeance! It is for us, servants of Bowanee, to draw towards us, by seducing wiles, all whose zeal, courage, and audacity may be useful to the cause. Let us rival each other in devotion and sacrifices; let us lend each other strength, help, support! That all who are not with us may be our prey, let us stand alone in the midst of all, against all, and in spite of all. For us, there must be neither country nor family. Our family is composed of our brethren; our country is the world."

This kind of savage eloquence made a deep impression on the negro and the Indian, over whom Faringhea generally exercised considerable influence, his intellectual powers being very superior to theirs, though they were themselves two of the most eminent chiefs of this bloody association. "Yes, you are right, brother!" cried the Indian, sharing the enthusiasm of Faringhea; "the world is ours. Even here, in Java, let us leave some trace of our passage. Before we depart, let us establish the good work in this island; it will increase quickly, for here also is great misery, and the Dutch are rapacious as the English. Brother, I have seen in the marshy rice-fields of this island, always fatal to those who cultivate them, men whom absolute want forced to the deadly task - they were livid as corpses - some of them worn out with sickness, fatigue, and hunger, fell - never to rise again. Brothers, the good work will prosper in this country!"

"The other evening," said the half-caste, "I was on the banks of the lake, behind a rock; a young woman came there - a few rags hardly covered her lean and sun-scorched body - in her arms she held a little child, which she pressed weeping to her milkless breast. She kissed it three times, and said to it: 'You, at least, shall not be so unhappy as your father' - and she threw it into the lake. It uttered one wail, and disappeared. On this cry, the alligators, hidden amongst the reeds, leaped joyfully into the water. There are mothers here who kill their children out of pity. - Brothers, the good work will prosper in this country!"

"This morning," said the negro, "whilst they tore the flesh of one of his black slaves with whips, a withered old merchant of Batavia left his country-house to come to the town. Lolling in his palanquin, he received, with languid indolence, the sad caresses of two of those girls, whom he had bought, to people his harem, from parents too poor to give them food. The palanquin, which held this little old man, and the girls, was carried by twelve young and robust men. There are here, you see, mothers who in their misery sell their own daughters - slaves that are scourged - men that carry other men, like beasts of burden. - Brothers, the good work will prosper in this country!"

"Yes, in this country - and in every land of oppression, distress, corruption, and slavery."

"Could we but induce Djalma to join us, as Mahal the Smuggler advised," said the Indian, "our voyage to Java would doubly profit us; for we should then number among our band this brave and enterprising youth, who has so many motives to hate mankind."

"He will soon be here; let us envenom his resentments."

"Remind him of his father's death!"

"Of the massacre of his people!"

"His own captivity!"

"Only let hatred inflame his heart, and he will be ours."

The negro, who had remained for some time lost in thought, said suddenly: "Brothers, suppose Mahal the Smuggler were to betray us?"

"He" cried the Hindoo, almost with indignation; "he gave us an asylum on board his bark; he secured our flight from the Continent; he is again to take us with him to Bombay, where we shall find vessels for America, Europe, Africa."

"What interest would Mahal have to betray us?" said Faringhea. "Nothing could save him from the vengeance of the sons of Bowanee, and that he knows."

"Well," said the black, "he promised to get Djalma to come hither this evening, and, once amongst us, he must needs be our own."

"Was it not the Smuggler who told us to order the Malay to

enter the ajoupa of Djalma, to surprise him during his sleep, and, instead of killing him as he might have done, to trace the name of Bowanee upon his arm? Djalma will thus learn to judge of the resolution, the cunning and obedience of our brethren, and he will understand what he has to hope or fear from such men. Be it through admiration or through terror, he must become one of us."

"But if he refuses to join us, notwithstanding the reasons he has to hate mankind?"

"Then - Bowanee will decide his fate," said Faringhea, with a gloomy look; "I have my plan."

"But will the Malay succeed in surprising Djalma during his sleep?" said the negro.

"There is none nobler, more agile, more dexterous, than the Malay," said Faringhea. "He once had the daring to surprise in her den a black panther, as she suckled her cub. He killed the dam, and took away the young one, which he afterwards sold to some European ship's captain."

"The Malay has succeeded!" exclaimed the Indian, listening to a singular kind of hoot, which sounded through the profound silence of the night and of the woods.

"Yes, it is the scream of the vulture seizing its prey," said the negro, listening in his turn; "it is also the signal of our brethren, after they have seized their prey."

In a few minutes, the Malay appeared at the door of the hut. He had wound around him a broad length of cotton, adorned with bright colored stripes.

"Well," said the negro, anxiously; "have you succeeded?"

"Djalma must bear all his life the mark of the good work," said the Malay, proudly. "To reach him, I was forced to offer up to

Bowanee a man who crossed my path - I have left his body under the brambles, near the ajoupa. But Djalma is marked with the sign. Mahal the Smuggler was the first to know it."

"And Djalma did not awake?" said the Indian, confounded by the Malay's adroitness.

"Had he awoke," replied the other, calmly, "I should have been a dead man - as I was charged to spare his life."

"Because his life may be more useful to us than his death," said the half-caste. Then, addressing the Malay, he added: "Brother, in risking life for the good work, you have done to-day what we did yesterday, what we may do again to-morrow. This time, you obey; another you will command."

"We all belong to Bowanee," answered the Malay. "What is there yet to do? - I am ready." Whilst he thus spoke, his face was turned towards the door of the hut; on a sudden, he said in a low voice: "Here is Djalma. He approaches the cabin. Mahal has not deceived us."

"He must not see me yet," said Faringhea, retiring to an obscure corner of the cabin, and hiding himself under a mat; "try to persuade him. If he resists - I have my project."

Hardly had Faringhea disappeared, saying these words, when Djalma arrived at the door of the hovel. At sight of those three personages with their forbidding aspect, Djalma started in surprise. But ignorant that these men belonged to the Phansegars, and knowing that, in a country where there are no inns, travellers often pass the night under a tent, or beneath the shelter of some ruins, he continued to advance towards them. After the first moment, he perceived by the complexion and the dress of one of these men, that he was an Indian, and he accosted him in the Hindoo language: "I thought to have found here a European - a Frenchman -"

"The Frenchman is not yet come," replied the Indian; "but he will not be long."

Guessing by Djalma's question the means which Mahal had employed to draw him into the snare, the Indian hoped to gain time by prolonging his error.

"You knew this Frenchman?" asked Djalma of the Phansegar.

"He appointed us to meet here, as he did you," answered the Indian.

"For what?" inquired Djalma, more and more astonished.

"You will know when he arrives."

"General Simon told you to be at this place?"

"Yes, General Simon," replied the Indian.

There was a moment's pause, during which Djalma sought in vain to explain to himself this mysterious adventure. "And who are you?" asked he, with a look of suspicion; for the gloomy silence of the Phansegar's two companions, who stared fixedly at each other, began to give him some uneasiness.

"We are yours, if you will be ours," answered the Indian.

"I have no need of you - nor you of me."

"Who knows?"

"I know it."

"You are deceived. The English killed your father, a king; made you a captive; proscribed you, you have lost all your possessions."

At this cruel reminder, the countenance of Djalma darkened. He started, and a bitter smile curled his lip. The

Phansegar continued:

"Your father was just and brave - beloved by his subjects - they called him 'Father of the Generous,' and he was well named. Will you leave his death unavenged? Will the hate, which gnaws at your heart, be without fruit?"

"My father died with arms in his hand. I revenged his death on the English whom I killed in war. He, who has since been a father to me, and who fought also in the same cause, told me, that it would now be madness to attempt to recover my territory from the English. When they gave me my liberty, I swore never again to set foot in India - and I keep the oaths I make."

"Those who despoiled you, who took you captive, who killed your father - were men. Are there not other men, on whom you can avenge yourself! Let your hate fall upon them!"

"You, who speak thus of men, are not a man!"

"I, and those who resemble me, are more than men. We are, to the rest of the human race, what the bold hunter is to the wild beasts, which they run down in the forest. Will you be, like us, more than a man? Will you glut surely, largely, safely - the hate which devours your heart, for all the evil done you?"

"Your words become more and more obscure: I have no hatred in my heart," said Djalma. "When an enemy is worthy of me, I fight with him; when he is unworthy, I despise him. So that I have no hate - either for brave men or cowards."

"Treachery!" cried the negro on a sudden, pointing with rapid gesture to the door, for Djalma and the Indian had now withdrawn a little from it, and were standing in one corner of the hovel.

At the shout of the negro, Faringhea, who had not been perceived by Djalma, threw off abruptly the mat which covered him, drew his crease, started up like a tiger, and with one bound was out of the cabin. Then, seeing a body of soldiers advancing cautiously in a circle, he dealt one of them a mortal stroke, threw down two others, and disappeared in the midst of the ruins. All this passed so instantaneously, that, when Djalma turned round, to ascertain the cause of the negro's cry of alarm, Faringhea had already disappeared.

The muskets of several soldiers, crowding to the door, were immediately pointed at Djalma and the three Stranglers, whilst others went in pursuit of Faringhea. The negro, the Malay, and the Indian, seeing the impossibility of resistance, exchanged a few rapid words, and offered their hands to the cords, with which some of the soldiers had provided themselves.

The Dutch captain, who commanded the squad, entered the cabin at this moment. "And this other one?" said he, pointing out Djalma to the soldiers, who were occupied in binding the three Phansegars.

"Each in his turn, captain!" said an old sergeant. "We come to him next."

Djalma had remained petrified with surprise, not understanding what was passing round him; but, when he saw the sergeant and two soldiers approach with ropes to bind him, he repulsed them with violent indignation, and rushed towards the door where stood the officer. The soldiers, who had supposed that Djalma would submit to his fate with the same impassibility as his companions, were astounded by this resistance, and recoiled some paces, being struck in spite of themselves, with the noble and dignified air of the son of Kadja-sing.

"Why would you bind me like these men?" cried Djalma, addressing himself in Hindostanee to the officer, who understood that language from his long service in the Dutch colonies.

"Why would we bind you, wretch? - because you form part of this band of assassins. What?" added the officer in Dutch, speaking to the soldiers, "are you afraid of him? - Tie the cord tight about his wrists; there will soon be another about his neck."

"You are mistaken," said Djalma, with a dignity and calmness which astonished the officer; "I have hardly been in this place a quarter of an hour - I do not know these men. I came here to meet a Frenchman."

"Not a Phansegar like them? - Who will believe the falsehood?"

"Them!" cried Djalma, with so natural a movement and expression of horror, that with a sign the officer stopped the soldiers, who were again advancing to bind the son of Kadja-sing; "these men form part of that horrible band of murderers! and you accuse me of being their accomplice! - Oh, in this case, sir! I am perfectly at ease," said the young man, with a smile of disdain.

"It will not be sufficient to say that you are tranquil," replied the officer; "thanks to their confessions, we now know by what mysterious signs to recognize the Thugs."

"I repeat, sir, that I hold these murderers in the greatest horror, and that I came here -"

The negro, interrupting Djalma, said to the officer with a ferocious joy: "You have hit it; the sons of the good work do know each other by marks tattooed on their skin. For us, the hour has come - we give our necks to the cord. Often enough have we twined it round the necks of those who served not with us the good work. Now, look at our arms, and look at the arms of this youth!"

The officer, misinterpreting the words of the negro, said to Djalma: "It is quite clear, that if, as this negro tells us, you do not bear on your arm the mysterious symbol - (we are going to assure ourselves of the fact), and if you can explain your presence here in a satisfactory manner, you may be at liberty within two hours."

"You do not understand me," said the negro to the officer; "Prince Djalma is one of us, for he bears on his left arm the name of Bowanee."

"Yes! he is like us, a son of Kale!" added the Malay.

"He is like us, a Phansegar," said the Indian.

The three men, irritated at the horror which Djalma had manifested on learning that they were Phansegars, took a savage pride in making it believed that the son of Kadja-sing belonged to their frightful association.

"What have you to answer?" said the officer to Djalma. The latter again gave a look of disdainful pity, raised with his right hand his long, wide left sleeve, and displayed his naked arm.

"What audacity!" cried the officer, for on the inner part of the fore arm, a little below the bend, the name of the Bowanee, in bright red Hindoo characters, was distinctly visible. The officer ran to the Malay, and uncovered his arm; he saw the same word, the same signs. Not yet satisfied, he assured himself that the negro and the Indian were likewise so marked.

"Wretch!" cried he, turning furiously towards Djalma; "you inspire even more horror than your accomplices. Bind him like a cowardly assassin," added he to the soldiers; "like a cowardly assassin, who lies upon the brink of the grave, for his execution will not be long delayed."

Struck with stupor, Djalma, who for some moments had kept his eye riveted on the fatal mark, was unable to pronounce a word, or make the least movement: his powers of thought seemed to fail him, in presence of this incomprehensible fact.

"Would you dare deny this sign?" said the officer to him, with indignation.

"I cannot deny what I see - what is," said Djalma, quite overcome.

"It is lucky that you confess at last," replied the officer. "Soldiers, keep watch over him and his accomplices - you answer for them."

Almost believing himself the sport of some wild dream. Djalma offered no resistance, but allowed himself to be bound and removed with mechanical passiveness. The officer, with part of his soldiers, hoped still to discover Faringhea amongst the ruins; but his search was vain, and, after spending an hour in fruitless endeavors, he set out for Batavia, where the escort of the prisoners had arrived before him.

Some hours after these events, M. Joshua van Dael thus finished his long despatch, addressed to M. Rodin, of Paris:

"Circumstances were such, that I could not act otherwise; and, taking all into consideration, it is a very small evil for a great good. Three murderers are delivered over to justice, and the temporary arrest of Djalma will only serve to make his innocence shine forth with redoubled luster.

"Already this morning I went to the governor, to protest in favor of our young prince. 'As it was through me,' I said, 'that those three great criminals fell into the hands of the authorities, let them at least show me some gratitude, by doing everything to render clear as day the innocence of Prince Djalma, so interesting by reason of his misfortunes and noble qualities. Most certainly,' I added, 'when I came yesterday to inform the governor, that the Phansegars would be found assembled in the ruins of Tchandi, I was far from anticipating that any one would confound with those wretches the adopted son of General Simon, an excellent man, with whom I have had for some time the most honorable relations. We must, then, at any cost, discover the inconceivable mystery that has placed Djalma in this dangerous position;' and, I continued, 'so convinced am I of his innocence, that, for his own sake, I would not ask for any favor on his behalf. He will have sufficient courage and dignity to wait patiently in prison for the day of justice.' In all this, you see, I spoke nothing but the truth, and had not to reproach myself with the least deception, for nobody in the world is more convinced than I am of Djalma's innocence.

"The governor answered me as I expected, that morally he felt as certain as I did of the innocence of the young prince, and would treat him with all possible consideration; but that it was necessary for justice to have its course, because it would be the only way of demonstrating the falsehood of the accusation, and discovering by what unaccountable fatality that mysterious sign was tattooed upon Djalma's arm.

"Mahal the Smuggler, who alone could enlighten justice on this subject, will in another hour have quitted Batavia, to go on board the 'Ruyter,' which will take him to Egypt; for he has a note from me to the captain, to certify that he is the person for whom I engaged and paid the passage. At the same time, he will be the bearer of this long despatch, for the 'Ruyter' is to sail in an hour, and the last letter-bag for Europe was made up yesterday evening. But I wished to see the governor this morning, before closing the present.

"Thus, then, is Prince Djalma enforced detained for a month, and, this opportunity of the 'Ruyter' once lost, it is materially impossible that the young Indian can be in France by the 13th of next February. You see, therefore, that, even as you ordered, so have I acted according to the means at my disposal - considering only the end which justifies them - for you tell me a great interest of the society is concerned.

"In your hands, I have been what we all ought to be in the hands of our superiors - a mere instrument: since, for the greater glory of God, we become corpses with regard to the will.[7] Men may deny our unity and power, and the times appear opposed to us; but circumstances only change; we are ever the same.

"Obedience and courage, secrecy and patience, craft and audacity, union and devotion - these become us, who have the world for our country, our brethren for family, Rome for our Queen!

"J. V."

About ten o'clock in the morning, Mahal the Smuggler set out with this despatch (sealed) in his possession, to board the "Ruyter." An hour later, the dead body of this same Mahal, strangled by Thuggee, lay concealed beneath some reeds on the edge of a desert strand, whither he had gone to take boat to join the vessel.

When at a subsequent period, after the departure of the steamship, they found the corpse of the smuggler, M. Joshua sought in vain for the voluminous packet, which he had entrusted to his care. Neither was there any trace of the note which Mahal was to have delivered to the captain of the "Ruyter," in order to be received as passenger.

Finally, the searches and bushwhacking ordered throughout the country for the purpose of discovering Faringhea, were of no avail. The dangerous chief of the Stranglers was never seen again in Java.

[7] It is known that the doctrine of passive and absolute obedience, the main-spring of the Society of Jesus, is summed up in those terrible words of the dying Loyola: "Every member of the Order shall be, in the hands of his superiors, even as a corpse (Perinde ac Cadaver)." - E. S.

CHAPTER XXIII

M. RODIN

Three months have elapsed since Djalma was thrown into Batavia Prison accused of belonging to the murderous gang of Megpunnas. The following scene takes place in France, at the commencement of the month of February, 1832, in Çardoville Manor House, an old feudal habitation standing upon the tall cliffs of Picardy, not far from Saint Valery, a dangerous coast on which almost every year many ships are totally wrecked, being driven on shore by the northwesters, which render the navigation of the Channel so perilous.

From the interior of the Castle is heard the howling of a violent tempest, which has arisen during the night; a frequent formidable noise, like the discharge of artillery, thunders in the distance, and is repeated by the echoes of the shore; it is the sea breaking with fury against the high rocks which are overlooked by the ancient Manor House.

It is about seven o'clock in the morning. Daylight is not yet visible through the windows of a large room situated on the ground-floor. In this apartment, in which a lamp is burning, a woman of about sixty years of age, with a simple and honest countenance, dressed as a rich farmer's wife of Picardy, is already occupied with her needle-work, notwithstanding the early hour. Close by, the husband of this woman, about the same age as herself, is seated at a large table, sorting and putting up in bags divers samples of wheat and oats. The face of this white-haired man is intelligent and open, announcing good sense and honesty, enlivened by a touch of rustic humor; he wears a shooting-jacket of green cloth, and long gaiters of tan-colored leather, which half conceal his black velveteen breeches.

The terrible storm which rages without renders still more agreeable the picture of this peaceful interior. A rousing fire burns in a broad chimney-place faced with white marble, and throws its joyous light on the carefully polished floor; nothing can be more cheerful than the old fashioned chintz hangings and curtains with red Chinese figures upon a white ground, and the panels over the door painted with pastoral scenes in the style of Watteau. A clock of Sevres china, and rosewood furniture inlaid with green - quaint and portly furniture, twisted into all sorts of grotesque shapes - complete the decorations of this apartment.

Out-doors, the gale continued to howl furiously, and sometimes a gust of wind would rush down the chimney, or shake the fastenings of the windows. The man who was occupied in sorting the samples of grain was M. Dupont, bailiff of Cardoville manor.

"Holy Virgin!" said his wife; "what dreadful weather, my dear! This M. Rodin, who is to come here this morning, as the Princess de Saint Dizier's steward announced to us, picked out a very bad day for it."

"Why, in truth, I have rarely heard such a hurricane. If M. Rodin has never seen the sea in its fury, he may feast his eyes to-day with the sight."

"What can it be that brings this M. Rodin, my dear?"

"Faith! I know nothing about it. The steward tells me in his letter to show M. Rodin the greatest attention, and to obey him as if he were my master. It will be for him to explain himself, and for me to execute his orders, since he comes on the part of the princess."

"By rights he should come from Mademoiselle Adrienne, as the land belongs to her since the death of the duke her father."

"Yes; but the princess being aunt to the young lady, her steward manages Mademoiselle Adrienne's affairs - so whether one or the other, it amounts to the same thing."

"May be M. Rodin means to buy the estate. Though, to be sure, that stout lady who came from Paris last week on purpose to see the chateau appeared to have a great wish for it."

At these words the bailiff began to laugh with a sly look.

"What is there to laugh at, Dupont?" asked his wife, a very good creature, but not famous for intelligence or penetration.

"I laugh," answered Dupont, "to think of the face and figure of that enormous woman: with such a look, who the devil would call themselves Madame de la Sainte-Colombe - Mrs. Holy Dove? A pretty saint, and a pretty dove, truly! She is round as a hogshead, with the voice of a town-crier; has gray moustachios like an old grenadier, and without her knowing it, I heard her say to her servant: 'Stir your stumps, my hearty!' - and yet she calls herself Sainte-Colombe!"

"How hard on her you are, Dupont; a body don't choose one's name. And, if she has a beard, it is not the lady's fault."

"No - but it is her fault to call herself Sainte-Colombe. Do you imagine it her true name? Ah, my poor Catherine, you are yet very green in some things."

"While you, my poor Dupont, are well read in slander! This lady seems very respectable. The first thing she asked for on arriving was the chapel of the Castle, of which she had heard speak. She even said that she would make some embellishments in it; and, when I told her we had no church in this little place, she appeared quite vexed not to have a curate in the village."

"Oh, to be sure! that's the first thought of your upstarts - to play the great lady of the parish, like your titled people."

"Madame de la Sainte-Colombe need not play the great lady, because she is one."

"She! a great lady? Oh, lor'!"

"Yes - only see how she was dressed, in scarlet gown, and violet gloves like a bishop's; and, when she took off her bonnet, she had a diamond band round her head-dress of false, light hair, and diamond ear-drops as large as my thumb, and diamond rings on every finger! None of your tuppenny beauties would wear so many diamonds in the middle of the day."

"You are a pretty judge!"

"That is not all."

"Do you mean to say there's more?"

"She talked of nothing but dukes, and marquises, and counts, and very rich gentlemen, who visit at her house, and are her most intimate friends; and then, when she saw the summer house in the park, half-burnt by the Prussians, which our late master never rebuilt, she asked, 'What are those ruins there?' and I answered: 'Madame, it was in the time of the Allies that the pavilion was burnt.' - 'Oh, my clear,' cried she; 'our allies, good, dear allies! they and the Restoration began my fortune!' So you see, Dupont, I said to myself directly: 'She was no doubt one of the noble women who fled abroad -'"

"Madame de la Sainte-Colombe!" cried the bailiff, laughing heartily. "Oh, my poor, poor wife!"

"Oh, it is all very well; but because you have been three years at Paris, don't think yourself a conjurer!"

"Catherine, let's drop it: you will make me say some folly, and there are certain things which dear, good creatures like you need never know."

"I cannot tell what you are driving at, only try to be less slanderous - for, after all, should Madame de la Sainte-Colombe buy the estate, will you be sorry to remain as her bailiff, eh?"

"Not I - for we are getting old, my good Catherine; we have lived here twenty years, and we have been too honest to provide for our old days by pilfering - and truly, at our age, it would be hard to seek another place, which perhaps we should not find. What I regret is, that Mademoiselle Adrienne should not keep the land; it seems that she wished to sell it, against the will of the princess."

"Good gracious, Dupont! is it not very extraordinary that Mademoiselle Adrienne should have the disposal of her large fortune so early in life?"

"Faith! simple enough. Our young lady, having no father or mother, is mistress of her property, besides having a famous little will of her own. Dost remember, ten years ago, when the count brought her down here one summer? - what an imp of mischief! and then what eyes! eh? - how they sparkled, even then!"

"It is true that Mademoiselle Adrienne had in her look - an expression - a very uncommon expression for her age."

"If she has kept what her witching, luring face promised, she must be very pretty by this time, notwithstanding the peculiar color of her hair - for, between ourselves, if she had been a tradesman's daughter, instead of a young lady of high birth, they would have called it red."

"There again! more slander."

"What! against Mademoiselle Adrienne? Heaven forbid - I always thought that she would be as good as pretty, and it is not speaking ill of her to say she has red hair. On the contrary, it always appears to me so fine, so bright, so sunny, and to suit so well her snowy complexion and black eyes, that in truth I would not have had it other than it was; and I am sure, that now this very color of her hair, which would be a blemish in any one else, must only add to the charm of Mademoiselle Adrienne's face. She must have such a sweet vixen look!"

"Oh! to be candid, she really was a vixen - always running about the park, aggravating her governess, climbing the trees - in fact, playing all manner of naughty tricks."

"I grant you, Mademoiselle Adrienne was a chip of the old block; but then what wit, what engaging ways, and above all, what a good heart!"

"Yes - that she certainly had. Once I remember she gave her shawl and her new merino frock to a poor little beggar girl, and came back to the house in her petticoat, and bare arms."

"Oh, an excellent heart - but headstrong - terribly headstrong!"

"Yes - that she was; and 'tis likely to finish badly, for it seems that she does things at Paris - oh! such things - "

"What things?"

"Oh, my dear; I can hardly venture - "

"Fell, but what are they?"

"Why," said the worthy dame, with a sort of embarrassment and confusion, which showed how much she was shocked by such enormities, "they say, that Mademoiselle Adrienne never sets foot in a church, but lives in a kind of heathen temple in her aunt's garden, where she has masked women to dress her up like a goddess, and scratches them very often, because she gets tipsy - without mentioning, that every night she plays on a hunting horn of massive gold - all which causes the utmost grief and despair to her poor aunt the princess."

Here the bailiff burst into a fit of laughter, which interrupted his wife.

"Now tell me," said he, when this first access of hilarity was over, "where did you get these fine stories about Mademoiselle Adrienne?"

"From Rene's wife, who went to Paris to look for a child to nurse; she called at Saint-Dizier House, to see Madame Grivois, her godmother. - Now Madame Grivois is first bedchamber woman to the princess - and she it was who told her all this - and surely she ought to know, being in the house."

"Yes, a fine piece of goods that Grivois! once she was a regular bad 'un, but now she professes to be as over-nice as her mistress; like master like man, they say. The princess herself, who is now so stiff and starched, knew how to carry on a lively game in her time. Fifteen years ago, she was no such prude: do you remember that handsome colonel of hussars, who was in garrison at Abbeville? an exiled noble who had served in Russia, whom the Bourbons gave a regiment on the Restoration?"

"Yes, yes - I remember him; but you are really too backbiting."

"Not a bit - I only speak the truth. The colonel spent his whole time here, and every one said he was very warm with this same princess, who is now such a saint. Oh! those were the jolly times. Every evening, some new entertainment at the chateau. What a fellow that colonel was, to set things going; how well he could act a play! - I remember -"

The bailiff was unable to proceed. A stout maid-servant, wearing the costume and cap of Picardy, entered in haste, and thus addressed her mistress: "Madame, there is a person here that wants to speak to master; he has come in the postmaster's calash from Saint-Valery, and he says that he is M. Rodin."

"M. Rodin?" said the bailiff rising. "Show him in directly!"

A moment after, M. Rodin made his appearance. According to his custom, he was dressed even more than plainly. With an air of great humility, he saluted the bailiff and his wife, and at a sign from her husband, the latter withdrew. The cadaverous countenance of M. Rodin, his almost invisible lips, his little reptile eyes, half concealed by their flabby lids, and the sordid style of his dress, rendered his general aspect far from prepossessing; yet this man knew how, when it was necessary, to affect, with diabolical art, so much sincerity and good-nature - his words were so affectionate and subtly penetrating - that the disagreeable feeling of repugnance, which the first sight of him generally inspired, wore off little by little, and he almost always finished by involving his dupe or victim in the tortuous windings of an eloquence as pliant as it was honeyed and perfidious; for ugliness and evil have their fascination, as well as what is good and fair.

The honest bailiff looked at this man with surprise, when he thought of the pressing recommendation of the steward of the Princess de Saint Dizier; he had expected to see quite another sort of personage, and, hardly able to dissemble his astonishment, he said to him: "Is it to M. Rodin that I have the honor to speak?"

"Yes, sir; and here is another letter from the steward of the Princess de Saint-Dizier."

"Pray, sir, draw near the fire, whilst I just see what is in this letter. The weather is so bad," continued the bailiff, obligingly, "may I not offer you some refreshment?"

"A thousand thanks, my dear sir; I am off again in an hour."

Whilst M. Dupont read, M. Rodin threw inquisitive glances round the chamber; like a man of skill and experience, he had frequently drawn just and useful inductions from those little appearances, which, revealing a taste or habit, give at the same time some notion of a character; on this occasion, however, his curiosity was at fault.

"Very good, sir," said the bailiff, when he had finished reading; "the steward renews his recommendation, and tells me to attend implicitly to your commands."

"Well, sir, they will amount to very little, and I shall not trouble you long."

"It will be no trouble, but an honor."

"Nay, I know how much your time must be occupied, for, as soon as one enters this chateau, one is struck with the good order and perfect keeping of everything in it - which proves, my dear sir, what excellent care you take of it."

"Oh, sir, you flatter me."

"Flatter you? - a poor old man like myself has something else to think of. But to come to business: there is a room here which is called the Green Chamber?"

"Yes, sir; the room which the late Count-Duke de Cardoville used for a study."

"You will have the goodness to take me there."

"Unfortunately, it is not in my power to do so. After the death of the Count-Duke, and when the seals were removed, a number of papers were shut up in a cabinet in that room, and the lawyers took the keys with them to Paris."

"Here are those keys," said M. Rodin, showing to the bailiff a large and a small key tied together.

"Oh, sir! that is different. You come to look for papers?"

"Yes - for certain papers - and also far a small mahogany casket, with silver clasps - do you happen to know it?"

"Yes, sir; I have often seen it on the count's writing-table. It must be in the large, lacquered cabinet, of which you have the key."

"You will conduct me to this chamber, as authorized by the Princess de Saint-Dizier?"

"Yes, sir; the princess continues in good health?"

"Perfectly so. She lives altogether above worldly things."

"And Mademoiselle Adrienne?"

"Alas, my dear sir!" said M. Rodin, with a sigh of deep contrition and grief.

"Good heaven, sir! has any calamity happened to Mademoiselle Adrienne?"

"In what sense do you mean it?"

"Is she ill?"

"No, no - she is, unfortunately, as well as she is beautiful."

"Unfortunately!" cried the bailiff, in surprise.

"Alas, yes! for when beauty, youth, and health are joined to an evil spirit of revolt and perversity - to a character which certainly has not its equal upon earth - it would be far better to be deprived of those dangerous advantages, which only become so many causes of perdition. But I conjure you, my dear sir, let us talk of something else: this subject is too painful," said M. Rodin, with a voice of deep emotion, lifting the tip of his little finger to the corner of his right eye, as if to stop a rising tear.

The bailiff did not see the tear, but he saw the gesture, and he was struck with the change in M. Rodin's voice. He answered him, therefore, with much sympathy: "Pardon my indiscretion, sir; I really did not know -"

"It is I who should ask pardon for this involuntary display of feeling - tears are so rare with old men - but if you had seen, as I have, the despair of that excellent princess, whose only fault has been too much kindness, too much weakness, with regard to her niece - by which she has encouraged her - but, once more, let us talk of something else, my dear sir!"

After a moment's pause, during which M. Rodin seemed to recover from his emotion, he said to Dupont: "One part of my mission, my dear sir - that which relates to the Green Chamber - I have now told you; but there is yet another. Before coming to it, however, I must remind you of a circumstance you have perhaps forgotten - namely, that some fifteen or sixteen years ago, the Marquis d'Aigrigny, then colonel of the hussars in garrison at Abbeville, spent some time in this house."

"Oh, sir! what a dashing officer was there! It was only just now, that I was talking about him to my wife. He was the life of the house! - how well he could perform plays - particularly the character of a scapegrace. In the Two Edmonds, for instance, he would make you die with laughing, in that part of a drunken soldier - and then, with what a charming voice he sang Joconde, sir - better than they could sing it at Paris!"

Rodin, having listened complacently to the bailiff, said to him: "You doubtless know that, after a fierce duel he had with a furious Bonapartist, one General Simon, the Marquis d'Aigrigny (whose private secretary I have now the honor to be) left the world for the church."

"No, sir! is it possible? That fine officer!"

"That fine officer - brave, noble, rich, esteemed, and flattered - abandoned all those advantages for the sorry black gown; and, notwithstanding his name, position, high connections, his reputation as a great preacher, he is still what he was fourteen years ago - a plain abbe - whilst so many, who have neither his merit nor his virtues, are archbishops and cardinals."

M. Rodin expressed himself with so much goodness, with such an air of conviction, and the facts he cited appeared to be so incontestable, that M. Dupont could not help exclaiming: "Well, sir, that is splendid conduct!"

"Splendid? Oh, no!" said M. Rodin, with an inimitable expression of simplicity; "it is quite a matter of course when one has a heart like M. d'Aigrigny's. But amongst all his good qualities, he has particularly that of never forgetting worthy people - people of integrity, honor, conscience - and therefore, my dear M. Dupont, he has not forgotten you."

"What, the most noble marquis deigns to remember -"

"Three days ago, I received a letter from him, in which he mentions your name."

"Is he then at Paris?"

"He will be there soon, if not there now. He went to Italy about three months ago, and, during his absence, he received a very sad piece of news - the death of his mother, who was passing the autumn on one of the estates of the Princess de Saint-Dizier."

"Oh, indeed! I was not aware of it."

"Yes, it was a cruel grief to him; but we must all resign ourselves to the will of Providence!"

"And with regard to what subject did the marquis do me the honor to mention my name?"

"I am going to tell you. First of all, you must know that this house is sold. The bill of sale was signed the day before my departure from Paris."

"Oh, sir! that renews all my uneasiness."

"Pray, why?"

"I am afraid that the new proprietors may not choose to keep me as their bailiff."

"Now see what a lucky chance! It is just on that subject that I am going to speak to you."

"Is it possible?"

"Certainly. Knowing the interest which the marquis feels for you, I am particularly desirous that you should keep this place, and I will do all in my power to serve you, if -"

"Ah, sir!" cried Dupont, interrupting Rodin; "what gratitude do I not owe you! It is Heaven that sends you to me!'

"Now, my dear sir, you flatter me in your turn; but I ought to tell you, that I'm obliged to annex a small condition to my support."

"Oh, by all means! Only name it, sir - name it!"

"The person who is about to inhabit this mansion, is an old lady in every way worthy of veneration; Madame de la Sainte-Colombe is the name of this respectable -"

"What, sir?" said the bailiff, interrupting Rodin; "Madame de la Sainte Colombe the lady who has bought us out?"

"Do you know her?"

"Yes, sir, she came last week to see the estate. My wife persists that she is a great lady; but - between ourselves - judging by certain words that I heard her speak -"

"You are full of penetration, my dear M. Dupont. Madame de la Sainte Colombe is far from being a great lady. I believe she was neither more nor less than a milliner, under one of the wooden porticoes of the Palais Royal. You see, that I deal openly with you."

"And she boasted of all the noblemen, French and foreign, who used to visit her!"

"No doubt, they came to buy bonnets for their wives! However, the fact is, that, having gained a large fortune and, after being in youth and middle age - indifferent - alas! more than indifferent to the salvation of her soul - Madame de la Sainte-Colombe is now in a likely way to experience grace - which renders her, as I told you, worthy of veneration, because nothing is so respectable as a sincere repentance - always providing it to be lasting. Now to make the good work sure and effectual, we shall need your assistance, my dear M. Dupont."

"Mine, sir! what can I do in it?"

"A great deal; and I will explain to you how. There is no church in this village, which stands at an equal distance from either of two parishes. Madame de la Sainte-Colombe, wishing to make choice of one of the two clergymen, will naturally apply to you and Madame Dupont, who have long lived in these parts, for information respecting them."

"Oh! in that case the choice will soon be made. The incumbent of Danicourt is one of the best of men."

"Now that is precisely what you must not say to Madame de la

Sainte Colombe."

"How so?"

"You must, on the contrary, much praise, without ceasing, the curate of Roiville, the other parish, so as to decide this good lady to trust herself to his care."

"And why, sir, to him rather than to the other?"

"Why? - because, if you and Madame Dupont succeed in persuading Madame de la Sainte-Colombe to make the choice I wish, you will be certain to keep your place as bailiff. I give you my word of it, and what I promise I perform."

"I do not doubt, sir, that you have this power," said Dupont, convinced by Rodin's manner, and the authority of his words; "but I should like to know -"

"One word more," said Rodin, interrupting him; "I will deal openly with you, and tell you why I insist on the preference which I beg you to support. I should be grieved if you saw in all this the shadow of an intrigue. It is only for the purpose of doing a good action. The curate of Roiville, for whom I ask your influence, is a man for whom M. d'Aigrigny feels a deep interest. Though very poor, he has to support an aged mother. Now, if he had the spiritual care of Madame de la Sainte Colombe, he would do more good than any one else, because he is full of zeal and patience; and then it is clear he would reap some little advantages, by which his old mother might profit - there you see is the secret of this mighty scheme. When I knew that this lady was disposed to buy an estate in the neighborhood of our friend's parish, I wrote about it to the marquis; and he, remembering you, desired me to ask you to render him this small service, which, as you see, will not remain without a recompense. For I tell you once more, and I will prove it, that I have the power to keep you in your place as bailiff."

"Well, sir," replied Dupont, after a moment's reflection, "you are so frank and obliging, that I will imitate your sincerity. In the same degree that the curate of Danicourt is respected and loved in this country, the curate of Roiville, whom you wish me to prefer to him, isdreaded for his intolerance - and, moreover -"

"Well, and what more?"

"Why, then, they say -"

"Come, what do they say?"

"They say - he is a Jesuit."

Upon these words, M. Rodin burst into so hearty a laugh that the bailiff was quite struck dumb with amazement - for the countenance of M. Rodin took a singular expression when he laughed. "A Jesuit!" he repeated, with redoubled hilarity; "a Jesuit! - Now really, my dear M. Dupont, for a man of sense, experience, and intelligence, how can you believe such idle stories? - A Jesuit - are there such people as Jesuits? - in our time, above all, can you believe such romance of the Jacobins, hobgoblins of the old freedom lovers? - Come, come; I wager, you have read about them in the Constitutionnel!"

"And yet, sir, they say -"

"Good heavens! what will they not say? - But wise men, prudent men like you, do not meddle with what is said - they manage their own little matters, without doing injury to any one, and they never sacrifice, for the sake of nonsense, a good place, which secures them a comfortable provision for the rest of their days. I tell you frankly, however much I may regret it, that should you not succeed in getting the preference for my man, you will not remain bailiff here.

"But, sir," said poor Dupont, "it will not be my fault, if this lady, hearing a great deal in praise of the other curate, should prefer him to your friend."

"Ah! but if, on the other hand, persons who have long lived in the neighborhood - persons worthy of confidence, whom she will see every day - tell Madame de la Sainte-Colombe a great deal of good of my friend, and a great deal of harm of the other curate, she will prefer the former, and you will continue bailiff."

"But, sir - that would be calumny!" cried Dupont.

"Pshaw, my dear M. Dupont!" said Rodin, with an air of sorrowful and affectionate reproach, "how can you think me capable of giving you evil counsel? - I was only making a supposition. You wish to remain bailiff on this estate. I offer you the certainty of doing so - it is for you to consider and decide."

"But, sir -"

"One word more - or rather one more condition - as important as the other. Unfortunately, we have seen clergymen take advantage of the age and weakness of their penitents, unfairly to benefit either themselves or others: I believe our protege incapable of any such baseness - but, in order to discharge my responsibility - and yours also, as you will have contributed to his appointment - I must request that you will write to me twice a week, giving the most exact detail of all that you have remarked in the character, habits, connections, pursuits, of Madame de la Sainte Colombe - for the influence of a confessor, you see, reveals itself in the whole conduct of life, and I should wish to be fully edified by the proceedings of my friend, without his being aware of it - or, if anything blameable were to strike you, I should be immediately informed of it by this weekly correspondence."

"But, sir - that would be to act as a spy?" exclaimed the unfortunate bailiff.

"Now, my dear M. Dupont! how can you thus brand the sweetest, most wholesome of human desires - mutual confidence? - I ask of you nothing else - I ask of you to write to me confidentially the details of all that goes on here. On these two conditions, inseparable one from the other, you remain bailiff; otherwise, I shall be forced, with grief and regret, to recommend some one else to Madame de la Sainte-Colombe."

"I beg you, sir," said Dupont, with emotion, "Be generous without any conditions! - I and my wife have only this place to give us bread, and we are too old to find another. Do not expose our probity of forty years' standing to be tempted by the fear of want, which is so bad a counsellor!"

"My dear M. Dupont, you are really a great child: you must reflect upon this, and give me your answer in the course of a week."

"Oh, sir! I implore you -" The conversation was here interrupted by a loud report, which was almost instantaneously repeated by the echoes of the cliffs. "What is that?" said M. Rodin. Hardly had he spoken, when the same noise was again heard more distinctly than before.

"It is the sound of cannon," cried Dupont, rising; "no doubt a ship in distress, or signaling for a pilot."

"My dear," said the bailiffs wife, entering abruptly, "from the terrace, we can see a steamer and a large ship nearly dismasted - they are drifting right upon the shore - the ship is firing minute gulls - it will be lost."

"Oh, it is terrible!" cried the bailiff, taking his hat and preparing to go out, "to look on at a shipwreck, and be able to do nothing!"

"Can no help be given to these vessels?" asked M. Rodin.

"If they are driven upon the reefs, no human power can save

them; since the last equinox two ships have been lost on this coast."

"Lost with all on board? - Oh, very frightful," said M. Rodin.

"In such a storm, there is but little chance for the crew; no matter," said the bailiff, addressing his wife, "I will run down to the rocks with the people of the farm, and try to save some of them, poor creatures! - Light large fires in several rooms - get ready linen, clothes, cordials - I scarcely dare hope to save any, but we must do our best. Will you come with me, M. Rodin?"

"I should think it a duty, if I could be at all useful, but I am too old and feeble to be of any service," said M. Rodin, who was by no means anxious to encounter the storm. "Your good lady will be kind enough to show me the Green Chamber, and when I have found the articles I require, I will set out immediately for Paris, for I am in great haste."

"Very well, sir. Catherine will show you. Ring the big bell," said the bailiff to his servant; "let all the people of the farm meet me at the foot of the cliff, with ropes and levers."

"Yes, my dear," replied Catherine; "but do not expose yourself."

"Kiss me - it will bring me luck," said the bailiff; and he started at a full run, crying: "Quick! quick; by this time not a plank may remain of the vessels."

"My dear madam," said Rodin, always impassible, "will you be obliging enough to show me the Green Chamber?"

"Please to follow me, sir," answered Catherine, drying her tears - for she trembled on account of her husband, whose courage she well knew.

CHAPTER XXIV

THE TEMPEST

The sea is raging. Mountainous waves of dark green, marbled with white foam, stand out, in high, deep undulations, from the broad streak of red light, which extends along the horizon. Above are piled heavy masses of black and sulphurous vapor, whilst a few lighter clouds of a reddish gray, driven by the violence of the wind, rush across the murky sky.

The pale winter sun, before he quite disappears in the great clouds, behind which he is slowly mounting, casts here and there some oblique rays upon the troubled sea, and gilds the transparent crest of some of the tallest waves. A band of snow-white foam boils and rages as far as the eye can reach, along the line of the reefs that bristle on this dangerous coast.

Half-way up a rugged promontory, which juts pretty far into the sea, rises Cardoville Castle; a ray of the sun glitters upon its windows; its brick walls and pointed roofs of slate are visible in the midst of this sky loaded with vapors.

A large, disabled ship, with mere shreds of sail still fluttering from the stumps of broken masts, drives dead upon the coast. Now she rolls her monstrous hull upon the waves - now plunges into their trough. A flash is seen, followed by a dull sound, scarcely perceptible in the midst of the roar of the tempest. That gun is the last signal of distress from this lost vessel, which is fast forging on the breakers.

At the same moment, a steamer, with its long plume of black smoke, is working her way from east to west, making every effort to keep at a distance from the shore, leaving the breakers on her left. The dismasted ship, drifting towards the rocks, at the mercy of the wind and tide, must some time pass right ahead of the steamer.

Suddenly, the rush of a heavy sea laid the steamer upon her side; the enormous wave broke furiously on her deck; in a second the chimney was carried away, the paddle box stove in, one of the wheels rendered useless. A second white-cap, following the first, again struck the vessel amidships, and so increased the damage that, no longer answering to the helm, she also drifted towards the shore, in the same direction as the ship. But the latter, though further from the breakers, presented a greater surface to the wind and sea, and so gained upon the steamer in swiftness that a collision between the two vessels became imminent - a new clanger added to all the horrors of the now certain wreck.

The ship was an English vessel, the "Black Eagle," homeward bound from Alexandria, with passengers, who arriving from India and Java, via the Red Sea, had disembarked at the Isthmus of Suez, from on board the steamship "Ruyter." The "Black Eagle," quitting the Straits of Gibraltar, had gone to touch at the Azores. She headed thence for Portsmouth, when she was overtaken in the Channel by the northwester. The steamer was the "William Tell," coming from Germany, by way of the Elbe, and bound, in the last place, for Hamburg to Havre.

These two vessels, the sport of enormous rollers, driven along by tide and tempest, were now rushing upon the breakers with frightful speed. The deck of each offered a terrible spectacle; the loss of crew and passengers appeared almost certain, for before them a tremendous sea broke on jagged rocks, at the foot of a perpendicular cliff.

The captain of the "Black Eagle," standing on the poop,

holding by the remnant of a spar, issued his last orders in this fearful extremity with courageous coolness. The smaller boats had been carried away by the waves; it was in vain to think of launching the long-boat; the only chance of escape in case the ship should not be immediately dashed to pieces on touching the rocks, was to establish a communication with the land by means of a life-line - almost the last resort for passing between the shore and a stranded vessel.

The deck was covered with passengers, whose cries and terror augmented the general confusion. Some, struck with a kind of stupor, and clinging convulsively to the shrouds, awaited their doom in a state of stupid insensibility. Others wrung their hands in despair, or rolled upon the deck uttering horrible imprecations. Here, women knelt down to pray; there, others hid their faces in their hands, that they might not see the awful approach of death. A young mother, pale as a specter, holding her child clasped tightly to her bosom, went supplicating from sailor to sailor, and offering a purse full of gold and jewels to any one that would take charge of her son.

These cries, and tears, and terror contrasted with the stern and silent resignation of the sailors. Knowing the imminence of the inevitable danger, some of them stripped themselves of part of their clothes, waiting for the moment to make a last effort, to dispute their lives with the fury of the waves; others renouncing all hope, prepared to meet death with stoical indifference.

Here and there, touching or awful episodes rose in relief, if one may so express it, from this dark and gloomy background of despair.

A young man of about eighteen or twenty, with shiny black hair, copper colored complexion, and perfectly regular and handsome features, contemplated this scene of dismay and horror with that sad calmness peculiar to those who have often braved great perils; wrapped in a cloak, he leaned his back against the bulwarks, with his feet resting against one of the bulkheads. Suddenly, the unhappy mother, who, with her child in her arms, and gold in her hand, had in vain addressed herself to several of the mariners, to beg them to save her boy, perceiving the young man with the copper-colored complexion, threw herself on her knees before him, and lifted her child towards him with a burst of inexpressible agony. The young man took it, mournfully shook his head, and pointed to the furious waves - but, with a meaning gesture, he appeared to promise that he would at least try to save it. Then the young mother, in a mad transport of hope, seized the hand of the youth, and bathed it with her tears.

Further on, another passenger of the "Black Eagle," seemed animated by sentiments of the most active pity. One would hardly have given him five-and-twenty years of age. His long, fair locks fell in curls on either side of his angelic countenance. He wore a black cassock and white neck-band. Applying himself to comfort the most desponding, he went from one to the other, and spoke to them pious words of hope and resignation; to hear him console some, and encourage others, in language full of unction, tenderness, and ineffable charity, one would have supposed him unaware or indifferent to the perils that he shared.

On his fine, mild features, was impressed a calm and sacred intrepidity, a religious abstraction from every terrestrial thought; from time to time, he raised to heaven his large blue eyes, beaming with gratitude, love, and serenity, as if to thank God for having called him to one of those formidable trials in which the man of humanity and courage may devote himself for his brethren, and, if not able to rescue them at all, at least die with them, pointing to the sky. One might almost have taken him for an angel, sent down to render less cruel the strokes of inexorable fate.

Strange contrast! not far from this young man's angelic beauty, there was another being, who resembled an evil spirit!

Boldly mounted on what was left of the bowsprit, to which he held on by means of some remaining cordage, this man looked down upon the terrible scene that was passing on the deck. A grim, wild joy lighted up his countenance of a dead yellow, that tint peculiar to those who spring from the union of the white race with the East. He wore only a shirt and linen drawers; from his neck was suspended, by a cord, a cylindrical tin box, similar to that in which soldiers carry their leave of absence.

The more the danger augmented, the nearer the ship came to the breakers, or to a collision with the steamer, which she was now rapidly approaching - a terrible collision, which would probably cause the two vessels to founder before even they touched the rocks - the more did the infernal joy of this passenger reveal itself in frightful transports. He seemed to long, with ferocious impatience, for the moment when the work of destruction should be accomplished. To see him thus feasting with avidity on all the agony, the terror, and the despair of those around him, one might have taken him for the apostle of one of those sanguinary deities, who, in barbarous countries, preside over murder and carnage.

By this time the "Black Eagle," driven by the wind and waves, came so near the "William Tell" that the passengers on the deck of the nearly dismantled steamer were visible from the first-named vessel.

These passengers were no longer numerous. The heavy sea, which stove in the paddle-box and broke one of the paddles, had also carried away nearly the whole of the bulwarks on that side; the waves, entering every instant by this large opening, swept the decks with irresistible violence, and every time bore away with them some fresh victims.

Amongst the passengers, who seemed only to have escaped this danger to be hurled against the rocks, or crushed in the encounter of the two vessels, one group was especially worthy of the most tender and painful interest. Taking refuge abaft, a tall old man, with bald forehead and gray moustache, had lashed himself to a stanchion, by winding a piece of rope round his body, whilst he clasped in his arms, and held fast to his breast, two girls of fifteen or sixteen, half enveloped in a pelisse of reindeer-skin. A large, fallow, Siberian dog, dripping with water, and barking furiously at the waves, stood close to their feet.

These girls, clasped in the arms of the old man, also pressed close to each other; but, far from being lost in terror, they raised their eyes to heaven, full of confidence and ingenuous hope, as though they expected to be saved by the intervention of some supernatural power.

A frightful shriek of horror and despair, raised by the passengers of both vessels, was heard suddenly above the roar of the tempest. At the moment when, plunging deeply between two waves, the broadside of the steamer was turned towards the bows of the ship, the latter, lifted to a prodigious height on a mountain of water, remained, as it were, suspended over the "William Tell," during the second which preceded the shock of the two vessels.

There are sights of so sublime a horror, that it is impossible to describe them. Yet, in the midst of these catastrophes, swift as thought, one catches sometimes a momentary glimpse of a picture, rapid and fleeting, as if illumined by a flash of lightning.

Thus, when the "Black Eagle," poised aloft by the flood, was about to crash down upon the "William Tell," the young man with the angelic countenance and fair, waving locks bent over the prow of the ship, ready to cast himself into the sea to save some victim. Suddenly, he perceived on board the steamer, on which he looked down from the summit of the immense wave, the two girls extending their arms towards him in supplication. They appeared to recognize him, and gazed on him with a sort of ecstacy and religious homage!

For a second, in spite of the horrors of the tempest, in spite of the approaching shipwreck, the looks of those three beings met. The features of the young man were expressive of sudden and profound pity; for the maidens with their hands clasped in prayer, seemed to invoke him as their expected Saviour. The old man, struck down by the fall of a plank, lay helpless on the deck. Soon all disappeared together.

A fearful mass of water dashed the "Black Eagle" down upon the "William Tell," in the midst of a cloud of boiling foam. To the dreadful crash of the two great bodies of wood and iron, which splintering against one another, instantly foundered, one loud cry was added - a cry of agony and death - the cry of a hundred human creatures swallowed up at once by the waves!

And then - nothing more was visible!

A few moments after, the fragments of the two vessels appeared in the trough of the sea, and on the caps of the waves - with here and there the contracted arms, the livid and despairing faces of some unhappy wretches, striving to make their way to the reefs along the shore, at the risk of being crushed to death by the shock of the furious breakers.

CHAPTER XXV

THE SHIPWRECK

While the bailiff was gone to the sea-shore, to render help to those of the passengers who might escape from the inevitable shipwreck, M. Rodin, conducted by Catherine to the Green Chamber, had there found the articles that he was to take with him to Paris.

After passing two hours in this apartment, very indifferent to the fate of the shipwrecked persons, which alone absorbed the attention of the inhabitants of the Castle, Rodin returned to the chamber commonly occupied by the bailiff, a room which opened upon a long gallery. When he entered it he found nobody there. Under his arm he held a casket, with silver fastenings, almost black from age, whilst one end of a large red morocco portfolio projected from the breast-pocket of his half buttoned great coat.

Had the cold and livid countenance of the Abbe d'Aigrigny's secretary been able to express joy otherwise than by a sarcastic smile, his features would have been radiant with delight; for, just then, he was under the influence of the most agreeable thoughts. Having placed the casket upon a table, it was with marked satisfaction that he thus communed with himself:

"All goes well. It was prudent to keep these papers here till this moment, for one must always be on guard against the diabolical spirit of that Adrienne de Cardoville, who appears to guess instinctively what it is impossible she should know. Fortunately, the time approaches when we shall have no more need to fear her. Her fate will be a cruel one; it must be so. Those proud, independent characters are at all times our natural enemies - they are so by their very essence - how much more when they show themselves peculiarly hurtful and dangerous! As for La Sainte Colombe, the bailiff is sure to act for us; between what the fool calls his conscience, and the dread of being at his age deprived of a livelihood, he will not hesitate. I wish to have him because he will serve us better than a stranger; his having been here twenty years will prevent all suspicion on the part of that dull and narrow-minded woman. Once in the hands of our man at Roiville, I will answer for the result. The course of all such gross and stupid women is traced beforehand: in their youth, they serve the devil; in riper years, they make others serve him; in their old age, they are horribly afraid of him; and this fear must continue till she has left us the Chateau de Cardoville, which, from its isolated position, will make us an excellent college. All then goes well. As for the affair of the medals, the 13th of February approaches, without news from Joshua - evidently, Prince Djalma is still kept prisoner by the English in the heart of India, or I must have received letters from Batavia. The daughters of General Simon will be detained at Leipsic for at least a month longer. All our foreign relations are in the best condition. As for our internal affairs -"

Here M. Rodin was interrupted in the current of his reflections by the entrance of Madame Dupont, who was zealously engaged in preparations togive assistance in case of need.

"Now," said she to the servant, "light a fire in the next room; put this warm wine there; your master may be in every minute."

"Well, my dear madam," said Rodin to her, "do they hope to save any of these poor creatures?"

"Alas! I do not know, sir. My husband has been gone nearly two hours. I am terribly uneasy on his account. He is so courageous, so imprudent, if once he thinks he can be of any service."

"Courageous even to imprudence," said Rodin to himself, impatiently; "I do not like that."

"Well," resumed Catherine, "I have here at hand my hot linen, my cordials - heaven grant it may all be of use!"

"We may at least hope so, my dear madam. I very much regretted that my age and weakness did not permit me to assist your excellent husband. I also regret not being able to wait for the issue of his exertions, and to wish him joy if successful - for I am unfortunately compelled to depart, my moments are precious. I shall be much obliged if you will have the carriage got ready."

"Yes, Sir; I will see about it directly."

"One word, my dear, good Madame Dupont. You are a woman of sense, and excellent judgment. Now I have put your husband in the way to keep, if he will, his situation as bailiff of the estate -"

"Is it possible? What gratitude do we not owe you! Without this place what would become of us at our time of life?"

"I have only saddled my promise with two conditions - mere trifles - he will explain all that to you."

"Ah, sir! we shall regard you as our deliverer."

"You are too good. Only, on two little conditions -"

"If there were a hundred, sir we should gladly accept them. Think what we should be without this place - penniless - absolutely penniless!"

"I reckon upon you then; for the interest of your husband, you will try to persuade him."

"Missus! I say, missus! here's master come back," cried a servant, rushing into the chamber.

"Has he many with him?"

"No, missus; he is alone."

"Alone! alone?"

"Quite alone, missus."

A few moments after, M. Dupont entered the room; his clothes were streaming with water; to keep his hat on in the midst of the storm, he had tied it down to his head by means of his cravat, which was knotted under his chin; his gaiters were covered with chalky stains.

"There I have thee, my dear love!" cried his wife, tenderly embracing him. "I have been so uneasy!"

"Up to the present moment - THREE SAVED."

"God be praised, my dear M. Dupont!" said Rodin; "at least your efforts will not have been all in vain."

"Three, only three?" said Catherine. "Gracious heaven!"

"I only speak of those I saw myself, near the little creek of Goelands. Let us hope there may be more saved on other parts of the coast."

"Yes, indeed; happily, the shore is not equally steep in all parts."

"And where are these interesting sufferers, my dear sir?" asked Rodin, who could not avoid remaining a few instants longer.

"They are mounting the cliffs, supported by our people. As they cannot walk very fast, I ran on before to console my wife, and to take the necessary measures for their reception. First of all, my dear, you must get ready some women's clothes."

"There is then a woman amongst the persons saved?"

"There are two girls - fifteen or sixteen years of age at the most - mere children - and so pretty!"

"Poor little things!" said Rodin, with an affectation of interest.

"The person to whom they owe their lives is with them. He is a real hero!"

"A hero?"

"Yes; only fancy -"

"You can tell me all this by and by. Just slip on this dry warm dressing-gown, and take some of this hot wine. You are wet through."

"I'll not refuse, for I am almost frozen to death. I was telling you that the person who saved these young girls was a hero; and certainly his courage was beyond anything one could have imagined. When I left here with the men of the farm, we descended the little winding path, and arrived at the foot of the cliff - near the little creek of Goelands, fortunately somewhat sheltered from the waves by five or six enormous masses of rock stretching out into the sea. Well, what should we find there? Why, the two young girls I spoke of, in a swoon, with their feet still in the water, and their bodies resting against a rock, as though they had been placed there by some one, after being withdrawn from the sea."

"Dear children! it is quite touching!" said M. Rodin, raising, as usual, the tip of his little finger to the corner of his right eye, as though to dry a tear, which was very seldom visible.

"What struck me was their great resemblance to each other," resumed the bailiff; "only one in the habit of seeing them could tell the difference."

"Twin - sisters, no doubt," said Madame Dupont.

"One of the poor things," continued the bailiff, "held between her clasped hands a little bronze medal, which was suspended from her neck by a chain of the same material."

Rodin generally maintained a very stooping posture; but at these last words of the bailiff, he drew himself up suddenly, whilst a faint color spread itself over his livid cheeks. In any other person, these symptoms would have appeared of little consequence; but in Rodin, accustomed for long years to control and dissimulate his emotions, they announced no ordinary excitement. Approaching the bailiff, he said to him in a slightly agitated voice, but still with an air of indifference: "It was doubtless a pious relic. Did you see what was inscribed on this medal?"

"No, sir; I did not think of it."

"And the two young girls were like one another - very much like, you say?"

"So like, that one would hardly know which was which. Probably they are orphans, for they are dressed in mourning."

"Oh! dressed in mourning?" said M. Rodin, with another start.

"Alas! orphans so young!" said Madame Dupont, wiping her eyes.

"As they had fainted away, we carried them further on to a place where the sand was quite dry. While we were busy about this, we saw the head of a man appear from behind one of the rocks, which he was trying to climb, clinging to it by one hand; we ran to him, and luckily in the nick of time, for he was clean worn out, and fell exhausted into the arms of our men. It was of him I spoke when I talked of a hero; for, not content with having saved the two young girls by his admirable courage, he had attempted to rescue a third person, and had actually gone back amongst the rocks and breakers - but his strength failed him, and, without the aid of our men, he would certainly have been washed away from the ridge to which he clung."

"He must indeed be a fine fellow!" said Catherine.

Rodin, with his head bowed upon his breast, seemed quite indifferent to this conversation. The dismay and stupor, in which he had been plunged, only increased upon reflection. The two girls, who had just been saved, were fifteen years of age; were dressed in mourning; were so like, that one might be taken for the other; one of them wore round her neck a chain with a bronze medal; he could scarcely doubt that they were the daughters of General Simon. But how could those sisters be amongst the number of shipwrecked passengers? How could they have escaped from the prison at Leipsic? How did it happen, that he had not been informed of it? Could they have fled, or had they been set at liberty? How was it possible that he should not be apprise of such an event? But these secondary thoughts, which offered themselves in crowds to the mind of M. Rodin, were swallowed up in the one fact: "the daughters of General Simon are here!" - His plan, so laboriously laid, was thus entirely destroyed.

"When I speak of the deliverer of these young girls," resumed the bailiff, addressing his wife, and without remarking M. Rodin's absence of mind, "you are expecting no doubt to see a Hercules? - well, he is altogether the reverse. He is almost a boy in look, with fair, sweet face, and light, curling locks. I left him a cloak to cover him, for he had nothing on but his shirt, black knee-breeches, and a pair of black worsted stockings - which struck me as singular."

"Why, it was certainly not a sailor's dress."

"Besides, though the ship was English, I believe my hero is a Frenchman, for he speaks our language as well as we do. What brought the tears to my eyes, was to see the young girls, when they came to themselves. As soon as they saw him, they threw themselves at his feet, and seemed to look up to him and thank him, as one would pray. Then they cast their eyes around them, as if in search of some other person, and, having exchanged a few words, they fell sobbing into each other's arms."

"What a dreadful thing it is! How many poor creatures must have perished!"

"When we quitted the rocks, the sea had already cast ashore seven dead bodies, besides fragments of the wrecks, and packages. I spoke to some of the coast-guard, and they will remain all day on the look-out; and if, as I hope, any more should escape with life, they are to be brought here. But surely that is the sound of voices! - yes, it is our shipwrecked guests!"

The bailiff and his wife ran to the door of the room - that door, which opened on the long gallery - whilst Rodin, biting convulsively his flat nails, awaited with angry impatience the arrival of the strangers. A touching picture soon presented itself to his view.

From the end of the dark some gallery, only lighted on one side by several windows, three persons, conducted by a peasant, advanced slowly. This group consisted of the two maidens, and the intrepid young man to whom they owed their lives. Rose and Blanche were on either side of their deliverer, who, walking with great difficulty, supported himself lightly on their arms.

Though he was full twenty-five years of age, the juvenile countenance of this man made him appear younger. His long, fair hair, parted on the forehead, streamed wet and smooth over the collar of a large brown cloak, with which he had been covered. It would be difficult to describe the adorable expression of goodness in his pale, mild face, as pure as the most ideal creations of Raphael's pencil - for that divine artist alone could have caught the melancholy grace of those exquisite features, the serenity of that celestial look, from eyes limpid and blue as those of an archangel, or of a martyr ascended to the skies.

Yes, of a martyr! for a blood-red halo already encircled that beauteous head. Piteous sight to see! just above his light eyebrows, and rendered still more visible by the effect of the cold, a narrow cicatrix, from a wound inflicted many months before, appeared to encompass his fair forehead with a purple band; and (still more sad!) his hands had been cruelly pierced by a crucifixion - his feet had suffered the same injury - and, if he now walked with so much difficulty, it was that his wounds had reopened, as he struggled over the sharp rocks.

This young man was Gabriel, the priest attached to the foreign mission, the adopted son of Dagobert's wife. He was a priest and martyr - for, in our days, there are still martyrs, as in the time when the Caesars flung the early Christians to the lions and tigers of the circus.

Yes, in our days, the children of the people - for it is almost always amongst them that heroic and disinterested devotion may still be found - the children of the people, led by an honorable conviction, because it is courageous and sincere, go to all parts of the world, to try and propagate their faith, and brave both torture and death with the most unpretending valor.

How many of them, victims of some barbarous tribe, have perished, obscure and unknown, in the midst of the solitudes of the two worlds! - And for these humble soldiers of the cross, who have nothing but their faith and their intrepidity, there is never reserved on their return (and they seldom do return) the rich and sumptuous dignities of the church. Never does the purple or the mitre conceal their scarred brows and mutilated limbs; like the great majority of other soldiers, they die forgotten.[8]

In their ingenuous gratitude, the daughters of General Simon, as soon as they recovered their senses after the shipwreck, and felt themselves able to ascend the cliffs, would not leave to any other person the care of sustaining the faltering steps of him who had rescued them from certain death.

The black garments of Rose and Blanche streamed with water; their faces were deadly pale, and expressive of deep grief; the marks of recent tears were on their cheeks, and, with sad, downcast eyes, they trembled both from agitation and cold, as the agonizing thought recurred to them, that they should never again see Dagobert, their friend and guide; for it was to him that Gabriel had stretched forth a helping hand, to assist him to climb the rocks. Unfortunately the strength of both had failed, and the soldier had been carried away by a retreating wave.

The sight of Gabriel was a fresh surprise for Rodin, who had retired on one side, in order to observe all; but this surprise was of so pleasant a nature, and he felt so much joy in beholding the missionary safe after such imminent peril, that the painful impression, caused by the view of General Simon's daughters, was a little softened. It must not be forgotten, that the presence of Gabriel in Paris, on the 13th of February, was essential to the success of Rodin's projects.

The bailiff and his wife, who were greatly moved at sight of the orphans, approached them with eagerness. Just then a farm-boy entered the room, crying: "Sir! sir! good news - two more saved from the wreck!"

"Blessing and praise to God for it!" said the missionary.

"Where are they?" asked the bailiff, hastening towards the door.

"There is one who can walk, and is following behind me with Justin; the other was wounded against the rocks, and they are carrying him on a litter made of branches."

"I will run and have him placed in the room below," said the bailiff, as he went out. "Catherine, you can look to the young ladies."

"And the shipwrecked man who can walk - where is he?" asked the bailiff's wife.

"Here he is," said the peasant, pointing to some one who came rapidly along the gallery; "when he heard that the two young ladies were safe in the chateau - though he is old, and wounded in the head, he took such great strides, that it was all I could do to get here before him."

Hardly had the peasant pronounced these words, when Rose and Blanche, springing up by a common impulse, flew to the door. They arrived there at the same moment as Dagobert.

The soldier, unable to utter a syllable, fell on his knees at the threshold, and extended his arms to the daughters of General Simon; while Spoil-sport, running to them licked their hands.

But the emotion was too much for Dagobert; and, when he had clasped the orphans in his arms, his head fell backward, and he would have sunk down altogether, but for the care of the peasants. In spite of the observations of the bailiff's wife, on their state of weakness and agitation, the two young girls insisted on accompanying Dagobert, who was carried fainting into an adjoining apartment.

At sight of the soldier, Rodin's face was again violently contracted, for he had till then believed that the guide of General Simon's daughters was dead. The missionary, worn out with fatigue, was leaning upon a chair, and had not yet perceived Rodin.

A new personage, a man with a dead yellow complexion, now entered the room, accompanied by another peasant, who pointed out Gabriel to him. This man, who had just borrowed a smock-frock and a pair of trousers, approached the missionary, and said to him in French but with a foreign accent: "Prince Djalma has just been brought in here. His first word was to ask for you."

"What does that man say?" cried Rodin, in a voice of thunder; for, at the name of Djalma, he had sprung with one bound to Gabriel's side.

"M. Rodin!" exclaimed the missionary, falling back in surprise.

"M. Rodin," cried the other shipwrecked person; and from that moment, he kept his eye fixed on the correspondent of M. Van Dael.

"You here, sir?" said Gabriel, approaching Rodin with an air of deference, not unmixed with fear.

"What did that man say to you?" repeated Rodin, in an excited tone. "Did he not utter the name of Prince Djalma?"

"Yes, sir; Prince Djalma was one of the passengers on board the English ship, which came from Alexandria, and in which we have just been wrecked. This vessel touched at the Azores, where I then was; the ship that brought me from Charlestown having been obliged to put in there, and being likely to remain for some time, on account of serious damage, I embarked on board the 'Black Eagle,' where I met Prince Djalma. We were bound to Portsmouth, and from thence my intention was to proceed to France."

Rodin did not care to interrupt Gabriel. This new shock had completely paralyzed his thoughts. At length, like a man who catches at a last hope, which he knows beforehand to be vain, he said to Gabriel: "Can you tell me who this Prince Djalma is?"

"A young man as good as brave - the son of an East Indian king, dispossessed of his territory by the English."

Then, turning towards the other shipwrecked man, the missionary said to him with anxious interest: "How is the Prince? are his wounds dangerous?"

"They are serious contusions, but they will not be mortal," answered the other.

"Heaven be praised!" said the missionary, addressing Rodin; "here, you see, is another saved."

"So much the better," observed Rodin, in a quick, imperious tone.

"I will go see him," said Gabriel, submissively. "You have no orders to give me?"

"Will you be able to leave this place in two or three hours, notwithstanding your fatigue?"

"If it be necessary - yes."

"It is necessary. You will go with me."

Gabriel only bowed in reply, and Rodin sank confounded into a chair, while the missionary went out with the peasant. The man with the sallow complexion still lingered in a corner of the room, unperceived by Rodin.

This man was Faringhea, the half-caste, one of the three chiefs of the Stranglers. Having escaped the pursuit of the soldiers in the ruins of Tchandi, he had killed Mahal the Smuggler, and robbed him of the despatches written by M. Joshua Van Dael to Rodin, as also of the letter by which the smuggler was to have been received as passenger on board the "Ruyter." When Faringhea left the hut in the ruins of Tchandi, he had not been seen by Djalma; and the latter, when he met him on shipboard, after his escape (which we shall explain by and by), not knowing that he belonged to the sect of Phansegars, treated him during the voyage as a fellow-countryman.

Rodin, with his eye fixed and haggard, his countenance of a livid hue, biting his nails to the quick in silent rage, did not perceive the half caste, who quietly approached him and laying his hand familiarly on his shoulder, said to him: "Your name is Rodin?"

"What now?" asked the other, starting, and raising his head abruptly.

"Your name is Rodin?" repeated Faringhea.

"Yes. What do you want?"

"You live in the Rue du Milieu-des-Ursins, Paris?"

"Yes. But, once more, what do you want?"

"Nothing now, brother: hereafter, much!"

And Faringhea, retiring, with slow steps, left Rodin alarmed at what had passed; for this man, who scarcely trembled at anything, had quailed before the dark look and grim visage of the Strangler.

[8] We always remember with emotion the end of a letter written, two or three years ago, by one of these young and valiant missionaries, the son of poor parents in Beauce. He was writing to his mother from the heart of Japan, and thus concluded his letter: "Adieu, my dear mother! they say there is much danger where I am now sent to. Pray for me, and tell all our good neighbors that I think of them very often." These few words, addressed from the centre of Asia to poor peasants in a hamlet of France, are only the more touching from their very simplicity - E. S.

CHAPTER XXVI

THE DEPARTURE FOR PARIS

The most profound silence reigns throughout Cardoville House. The tempest has lulled by degrees, and nothing is heard from afar but the hoarse murmur of the waves, as they wash heavily the shore.

Dagobert and the orphans have been lodged in warm and comfortable apartments on the first-floor of the chateau. Djalma, too severely hurt to be carried upstairs, has remained in a room below. At the moment of the shipwreck, a weeping mother had placed her child in his arms. He had failed in the attempt to snatch this unfortunate infant from certain death, but his generous devotion had hampered his movements, and when thrown upon the rocks, he was almost dashed to pieces. Faringhea, who has been able to convince him of his affection, remains to watch over him.

Gabriel, after administering consolation to Djalma, has rescinded to the chamber allotted to him; faithful to the promise he made to Rodin, to be ready to set out in two hours, he has not gone to bed; but, having dried his clothes, he has fallen asleep in a large, high-backed arm-chair, placed in front of a bright coal-fire. His apartment is situated near those occupied by Dagobert and the two sisters.

Spoil-sport, probably quite at his ease in so respectable a dwelling, has quitted the door of Rose and Blanche's chamber, to lie down and warm himself at the hearth, by the side of which the missionary is sleeping. There, with his nose resting on his outstretched paws, he enjoys a feeling of perfect comfort and repose, after so many perils by land and sea. We will not venture to affirm, that he thinks habitually of poor old Jovial; unless we recognize as a token of remembrance on his part, his irresistible propensity to bite all the white horses he has met with, ever since the death of his venerable companion, though before, he was the most inoffensive of dogs with regard to horses of every color.

Presently one of the doors of the chamber opened, and the two sisters entered timidly. Awake for some minutes, they had risen and dressed themselves, feeling still some uneasiness with respect to Dagobert; though the bailiff's wife, after showing them to their room, had returned again to tell them that the village doctor found nothing serious in the hurt of the old soldier, still they hoped to meet some one belonging to the chateau, of whom they could make further inquiries about him.

The high back of the old-fashioned arm-chair, in which Gabriel was sleeping, completely screened him from view; but the orphans, seeing their canine friend lying quietly at his feet, thought it was Dagobert reposing there, and hastened towards him on tip-toe. To their great astonishment, they saw Gabriel fast asleep, and stood still in confusion, not daring to advance or recede, for fear of waking him.

The long, light hair of the missionary was no longer wet, and now curled naturally round his neck and shoulders; the paleness of his complexion was the more striking, from the contrast afforded by the deep purple of the damask covering of the arm-chair. His beautiful countenance expressed a profound melancholy, either caused by the influence of some painful dream, or else that he was in the habit of keeping down, when awake, some sad regrets, which revealed themselves without his knowledge when he was sleeping. Notwithstanding this appearance of bitter grief, his features preserved their character of angelic sweetness, and seemed endowed with an inexpressible charm, for nothing is more touching than suffering goodness. The two young girls cast down their eyes, blushed simultaneously, and exchanged anxious glances, as if to point out to each other the slumbering missionary.

"He sleeps, sister," said Rose in a low voice.

"So much the better," replied Blanche, also in a whisper, making a sign of caution; "we shall now be able to observe him well."

"Yes, for we durst not do so, in coming from the sea hither."

"Look! what a sweet countenance!"

"He is just the same as we saw him in our dreams."

"When he promised he would protect us."

"And he has not failed us."

"But here, at least, he is visible."

"Not as it was in the prison at Leipsic, during that dark night."

"And so - he has again rescued us."

"Without him, we should have perished this morning."

"And yet, sister, it seems to me, that in our dreams his countenance shone with light."

"Yes, you know it dazzled us to look at him."

"And then he had not so sad a mien."

"That was because he came then from heaven; now he is upon earth."

"But, sister, had he then that bright red scar round his forehead?"

"Oh, no! we should have certainly perceived it."

"And these other marks on his hands?"

"If he has been wounded, how can he be an archangel?"

"Why not, sister? If he received those wounds in preventing evil, or in helping the unfortunate, who, like us, were about to perish?"

"You are right. If he did not run any danger for those he protects, it would be less noble."

"What a pity that he does not open his eye!"

"Their expression is so good, so tender!"

"Why did he not speak of our mother, by the way?"

"We were not alone with him; he did not like to do so."

"But now we are alone."

"If we were to pray to him to speak to us?"

The orphans looked doubtingly at each other, with charming simplicity; a bright glow suffused their cheeks, and their young bosoms heaved gently beneath their black dresses.

"You are right. Let us kneel down to him."

"Oh, sister! our hearts beat so!" said Blanche, believing rightly, that Rose felt exactly as she did. "And yet it seems to do us good. It is as if some happiness were going to befall us."

The sisters, having approached the arm-chair on tip-toe, knelt down with clasped hands, one to the right the other to the left of the young priest. It was a charming picture. Turning their lovely faces towards him, they said in a low whisper, with a soft, sweet voice, well suited to their youthful appearance: "Gabriel! speak to us of our mother!"

On this appeal, the missionary gave a slight start, half-opened his eyes, and, still in a state of semi-consciousness, between sleep and waking, beheld those two beauteous faces turned towards him, and heard two gentle voices repeat his name.

"Who calls me?" said he, rousing himself, and raising his head.

"It is Blanche and Rose."

It was now Gabriel's turn to blush, for he recognized the young girls he had saved. "Rise, my sisters!" said he to them; "you should kneel only unto God."

The orphans obeyed, and were soon beside him, holding each other by the hand. "You know my name, it seems," said the missionary with a smile.

"Oh, we have not forgotten it!"

"Who told it you?"

"Yourself."

"I?"

"Yes - when you came from our mother."

"I, my sisters?" said the missionary, unable to comprehend the words of the orphans. "You are mistaken. I saw you to-day for the first time."

"But in our dreams?"

"Yes - do you not remember? - in our dreams."

"In Germany - three months ago, for the first time. Look at us well."

Gabriel could not help smiling at the simplicity of Rose and Blanche, who expected him to remember a dream of theirs; growing more and more perplexed, he repeated: "In your dreams?"

"Certainly; when you gave us such good advice."

"And when we were so sorrowful in prison, your words, which we remembered, consoled us, and gave us courage."

"Was it not you, who delivered us from the prison at Leipsic, in that dark night, when we were not able to see you?"

"I!"

"What other but you would thus have come to our help, and to that of our old friend?"

"We told him, that you would love him, because he loved us, although he would not believe in angels."

"And this morning, during the tempest, we had hardly any fear."

"Because we expected you."

"This morning - yes, my sisters - it pleased heaven to send me to your assistance. I was coming from America, but I have never been in Leipsic. I could not, therefore, have let you out of prison. Tell me, my sisters," added he, with a benevolent smile, "for whom do you take me?"

"For a good angel whom we have seen already in dreams, sent by our mother from heaven to protect us."

"My dear sisters, I am only a poor priest. It is by mere chance, no doubt, that I bear some resemblance to the angel you have seen in your dreams, and whom you could not see in any other manner - for angels are not visible to mortal eye.

"Angels are not visible?" said the orphans, looking sorrowfully at each other.

"No matter, my dear sisters," said Gabriel, taking them affectionately by the hand; "dreams, like everything else, come from above. Since the remembrance of your mother was mixed up with this dream, it is twice blessed."

At this moment a door opened, and Dagobert made his appearance. Up to this time, the orphans, in their innocent ambition to be protected by an archangel, had quite forgotten the circumstance that Dagobert's wife had adopted a forsaken child, who was called Gabriel, and who was now a priest and missionary.

The soldier, though obstinate in maintaining that his hurt was only a blank wound (to use a term of General Simon's), had allowed it to be carefully dressed by the surgeon of the village, and now wore a black bandage, which concealed one half of his forehead, and added to the natural grimness of his features. On entering the room, he was not a little surprised to see a stranger holding the hands of Rose and Blanche familiarly in his own. This surprise was natural, for Dagobert did not know that the missionary had saved the lives of the orphans, and had attempted to save his also.

In the midst of the storm, tossed about by the waves, and vainly striving to cling to the rocks, the soldier had only seen Gabriel very imperfectly, at the moment when, having snatched the sisters from certain death, the young priest had fruitlessly endeavored to come to his aid. And when, after the shipwreck, Dagobert had found the orphans in safety beneath the roof of the Manor House, he fell, as we have already stated, into a swoon, caused by fatigue, emotion, and the effects of his wound - so that he had again no opportunity of observing the features of the missionary.

The veteran began to frown from beneath his black bandage and thick, gray brows, at beholding a stranger so familiar with Rose and Blanche; but the sisters ran to throw themselves into his arms, and to cover him with filial caresses. His anger was soon dissipated by these marks of affection, though he continued, from time to time, to cast a suspicious glance at the missionary, who had risen from his seat, but whose countenance he could not well distinguish.

"How is your wound?" asked Rose, anxiously. "They told us it was not dangerous."

"Does it still pain?" added Blanche.

"No, children; the surgeon of the village would bandage me up in this manner. If my head was carbonadoes with sabre cuts, I could not have more wrappings. They will take me for an old milksop; it is only a blank wound, and I have a good mind to - " And therewith the soldier raised one of his hands to the bandage.

"Will you leave that alone?" cried Rose catching his arm. "How can you be so unreasonable - at your age?"

"Well, well! don't scold! I will do what you wish, and keep it on." Then, drawing the sisters to one end of the room, he said to them in a low voice, whilst he looked at the young priest from the corner of his eye: "Who is that gentleman who was holding your hands when I came in? He has very much the look of a curate. You see, my children, you must be on your guard; because -"

"He?" cried both sisters at once, turning towards Gabriel. "Without him, we should not now be here to kiss you."

"What's that?" cried the soldier, suddenly drawing up his tall figure, and gazing full at the missionary.

"It is our guardian angel," resumed Blanche.

"Without him," said Rose, "we must have perished this morning in the shipwreck."

"Ah! it is he, who -" Dagobert could say no more. With swelling heart, and tears in his eyes, he ran to the missionary, offered him both his hands, and exclaimed in a tone of gratitude impossible to describe: "Sir, I owe you the lives of these two children. I feel what a debt that service lays upon me. I will not say more - because it includes everything!"

Then, as if struck with a sudden recollection, he cried: "Stop! when I was trying to cling to a rock, so as not to be carried away by the waves, was it not you that held out your hand to me? Yes - that light hair - that youthful countenance - yes - it was certainly you - now I am sure of it!"

"Unhappily, sir, my strength failed me, and I had the anguish to see you fall back into the sea."

"I can say nothing more in the way of thanks than what I have already said," answered Dagobert, with touching simplicity: "in preserving these children you have done more for me than if you had saved my own life. But what heart and courage!" added the soldier, with admiration; "and so young, with such a girlish look!"

"And so," cried Blanche, joyfully, "our Gabriel came to your aid also?"

"Gabriel!" said Dagobert interrupting Blanche, and addressing himself to the priest. "Is your name Gabriel?"

"Yes, sir."

"Gabriel!" repeated the soldier, more and more surprised.

"And a priest!" added he.

"A priest of the foreign missions."

"Who - who brought you up?" asked the soldier, with increasing astonishment.

"An excellent and generous woman, whom I revere as the best of mothers: for she had pity on me, a deserted infant, and treated me ever as her son."

"Frances Baudoin - was it not?" said the soldier, with deep emotion.

"It was, sir," answered Gabriel, astonished in his turn. "But how do you know this?"

"The wife of a soldier, eh?" continued Dagobert.

"Yes, of a brave soldier - who, from the most admirable devotion, is even now passing his life in exile - far from his wife - far from his son, my dear brother - for I am proud to call him by that name -"

"My Agricola! - my wife! - when did you leave them?"

"What! is it possible! You the father of Agricola? - Oh! I knew not, until now," cried Gabriel, clasping his hands together, "I knew not all the gratitude that I owed to heaven!"

"And my wife! my child!" resumed Dagobert, in a trembling voice; "how are they? have you news of them?"

"The accounts I received, three months ago, were excellent."

"No; it is too much," cried Dagobert; "it is too much!" The veteran was unable to proceed; his feelings stifled his words, and fell back exhausted in a chair.

And now Rose and Blanche recalled to mind that portion of their father's letter which related to the child named Gabriel, whom the wife of Dagobert had adopted; then they also yielded to transports of innocent joy.

"Our Gabriel is the same as yours - what happiness!" cried Rose.

"Yes, my children! he belongs to you as well as to me. We have all our part in him." Then, addressing Gabriel, the soldier added with affectionate warmth: "Your hand, my brave boy! give me your hand!"

"Oh, sir! you are too good to me."

"Yes - that's it - thank me! - after all thou has done for us!"

"Does my adopted mother know of your return?" asked Gabriel, anxious to escape from the praises of the soldier.

"I wrote to her five months since, but said that I should come alone; there was a reason for it, which I will explain by and by. Does she still live in the Rue Brise-Miche? It was there Agricola was born."

"She still lives there."

"In that case, she must have received my letter. I wished to write to her from the prison at Leipsic, but it was impossible."

"From prison! Have you just come out of prison?"

"Yes; I come straight from Germany, by the Elbe and Hamburg, and I should be still at Leipsic, but for an event which the Devil must have had a hand in - a good sort of devil, though."

"What do you mean? Pray explain to me."

"That would be difficult, for I cannot explain it to myself. These little ladies," he added, pointing with a smile to Rose and Blanche, "pretended to know more about it than I did, and were continually repeating: 'It was the angel that came to our assistance, Dagobert - the good angel we told thee of - though you said you would rather have Spoil sport to defend us -'"

"Gabriel, I am waiting for you," said a stern voice, which made the missionary start. They all turned round instantly, whilst the dog uttered a deep growl.

It was Rodin. He stood in the doorway leading to the corridor. His features were calm and impassive, but he darted a rapid, piercing glance at the soldier and sisters.

"Who is that man?" said Dagobert, very little prepossessed in favor of Rodin, whose countenance he found singularly repulsive. "What the mischief does he want?"

"I must go with him," answered Gabriel, in a tone of sorrowful constraint. Then, turning to Rodin, he added: "A thousand pardons! I shall be ready in a moment."

"What!" cried Dagobert, stupefied with amazement, "going the very instant we have just met? No, by my faith! you shall not go. I have too much to tell you, and to ask in return. We will make the journey together. It will be a real treat for me."

"It is impossible. He is my superior, and I must obey him."

"Your superior? - why, he's in citizen's dress."

"He is not obliged to wear the ecclesiastical garb."

"Rubbish! since he is not in uniform, and there is no provost-marshal in your troop, send him to the - "

"Believe me, I would not hesitate a minute, if it were possible to remain."

"I was right in disliking the phi of that man," muttered Dagobert between his teeth. Then he added, with an air of impatience and vexation: "Shall I tell him that he will much oblige us by marching off by himself?"

"I beg you not to do so," said Gabriel; "it would be useless; I know my duty, and have no will but my superior's. As soon as you arrive in Paris, I will come and see you, as also my adopted mother, and my dear brother, Agricola."

"Well - if it must be. I have been a soldier, and know what subordination is," said Dagobert, much annoyed. "One must put a good face on bad fortune. So, the day after to-morrow, in the Rue Brise-Miche, my boy; for they tell me I can be in Paris by to-morrow evening, and we set out almost immediately. But I say - there seems to be a strict discipline with you fellows!"

"Yes, it is strict and severe," answered Gabriel, with a shudder, and a stifled sigh.

"Come, shake hands - and let's say farewell for the present. After all, twenty-four hours will soon pass away."

"Adieu! adieu!" replied the missionary, much moved, whilst he returned the friendly pressure of the veteran's hand.

"Adieu, Gabriel!" added the orphans, sighing also, and with tears in their eyes.

"Adieu, my sisters!" said Gabriel - and he left the room with Rodin, who had not lost a word or an incident of this scene.

Two hours after, Dagobert and the orphans had quitted the Castle for Paris, not knowing that Djalma was left at Cardoville, being still too much injured to proceed on his journey. The half-caste, Faringhea, remained with the young prince, not wishing, he said, to desert a fellow countryman.

We now conduct the reader to the Rue Brise-Miche, the residence of Dagobert's wife.

CHAPTER XXVII

DAGOBERT'S WIFE

The following scenes occur in Paris, on the morrow of the day when the shipwrecked travellers were received in Cardoville House.

Nothing can be more gloomy than the aspect of the Rue Brise-Miche, one end of which leads into the Rue Saint-Merry, and the other into the little square of the Cloister, near the church. At this end, the street, or rather alley - for it is not more than eight feet wide - is shut in between immense black, muddy dilapidated walls, the excessive height of which excludes both air and light; hardly, during the longest days of the year, is the sun able to throw into it a few straggling beams; whilst, during the cold damps of winter, a chilling fog, which seems to penetrate everything, hangs constantly above the miry pavement of this species of oblong well.

It was about eight o'clock in the evening; by the faint, reddish light of the street lamp, hardly visible through the haze, two men, stopping at the angle of one of those enormous walls, exchanged a few words together.

"So," said one, "you understand all about it. You are to watch in the street, till you see them enter No. 5."

"All right!" answered the other.

"And when you see 'em enter so as to make quite sure of the game, go up to Frances Baudoin's room -"

"Under the cloak of asking where the little humpbacked workwoman lives - the sister of that gay girl, the Queen of the Bacchanals."

"Yes - and you must try and find out her address also - from her humpbacked sister, if possible - for it is very important. Women of her feather change their nests like birds, and we have lost track of her."

"Make yourself easy; I will do my best with Hump, to learn where her sister hangs out."

"And, to give you steam, I'll wait for you at the tavern opposite the Cloister, and we'll have a go of hot wine on your return."

"I'll not refuse, for the night is deucedly cold."

"Don't mention it! This morning the water friz on my sprinkling-brush, and I turned as stiff as a mummy in my chair at the church-door. Ah, my boy! a distributor of holy water is not always upon roses!"

"Luckily, you have the pickings -"

"Well, well - good luck to you! Don't forget the Fiver, the little passage next to the dyer's shop."

"Yes, yes - all right!" and the two men separated.

One proceeded to the Cloister Square; the other towards the further end of the street, where it led into the Rue Saint-Merry. This latter soon found the number of the house he sought - a tall, narrow building, having, like all the other houses in the street, a poor and wretched appearance. When he saw he was right, the man commenced walking backwards and forwards in front of the door of No. 5.

If the exterior of these buildings was uninviting, the gloom and squalor of the interior cannot be described. The house No. 5 was, in a special degree, dirty and dilapidated. The water, which oozed from the wall, trickled down the dark and filthy staircase. On the second floor, a wisp of straw had been laid on the narrow landing-place, for wiping the feet on; but this straw, being now quite rotten, only served to augment the sickening odor, which arose from want of air, from damp, and from the putrid exhalations of the drains. The few openings, cut at rare intervals in the walls of the staircase, could hardly admit more than some faint rays of glimmering light.

In this quarter, one of the most populous in Paris, such houses as these, poor, cheerless, and unhealthy, are generally inhabited by the working classes. The house in question was of the number. A dyer occupied the ground floor; the deleterious vapors arising from his vats added to the stench of the whole building. On the upper stories, several artisans lodged with their families, or carried on their different trades. Up four flights of stairs was the lodging of Frances Baudoin, wife of Dagobert. It consisted of one room, with a closet adjoining, and was now lighted by a single candle. Agricola occupied a garret in the roof.

Old grayish paper, broken here and there by the cracks covered the crazy wall, against which rested the bed; scanty curtains, running upon an iron rod, concealed the windows; the brick floor, not polished, but often washed, had preserved its natural color. At one end of this room was a round iron stove, with a large pot for culinary purposes. On the wooden table, painted yellow, marbled with brown, stood a miniature house made of iron - a masterpiece of patience and skill, the work of Agricola Baudoin, Dagobert's son.

A plaster crucifix hung up against the wall, surrounded by several branches of consecrated box-tree, and various images of saints, very coarsely colored, bore witness to the habits of the soldier's wife. Between the windows stood one of those old walnut-wood presses, curiously fashioned, and almost black with time; an old arm-chair, covered with green cotton velvet (Agricola's first present to his mother), a few rush bottomed chairs, and a worktable on which lay several bags of coarse, brown cloth, completed the furniture of this room, badly secured by a worm-eaten door. The adjoining closet contained a few kitchen and household utensils.

Mean and poor as this interior may perhaps appear, it would not seem so to the greater number of artisans; for the bed was supplied with two mattresses, clean sheets, and a warm counterpane; the old-fashioned press contained linen; and, moreover, Dagobert's wife occupied all to herself a room as large as those in which numerous families, belonging to honest and laborious workmen, often live and sleep huddled together - only too happy if the boys and girls can have separate beds, or if the sheets and blankets are not pledged at the pawnbroker's.

Frances Baudoin, seated beside the small stove, which, in the cold and damp weather, yielded but little warmth, was busied in preparing her son Agricola's evening meal.

Dagobert's wife was about fifty years of age; she wore a close jacket of blue cotton, with white flowers on it, and a stuff petticoat; a white handkerchief was tied round her head, and fastened under the chin. Her countenance was pale and meagre, the features regular, and expressive of resignation and great kindness. It would have been difficult to find a better, a more courageous mother. With no resource but her labor, she had succeeded, by unwearied energy, in bringing up not only her own son Agricola, but also Gabriel, the poor deserted child, of whom, with admirable devotion, she had ventured to take charge.

In her youth, she had, as it were, anticipated the strength of later life, by twelve years of incessant toil, rendered lucrative by the most violent exertions, and accompanied by such privations as made it almost suicidal. Then (for it was a time of splendid wages, compared to the present), by sleepless nights and constant labor, she contrived to earn about two shillings (fifty sous) a day, and with this she managed to educate her son and her adopted child.

At the end of these twelve years, her health was ruined, and her strength nearly exhausted; but, at all events, her boys had wanted for nothing, and had received such an education as children of the people can obtain. About this time, M. Francois Hardy took Agricola as an apprentice, and Gabriel prepared to enter the priest's seminary, under the active patronage of M. Rodin, whose communications with the confessor of Frances Baudoin had become very frequent about the year 1820.

This woman (whose piety had always been excessive) was one of those simple natures, endowed with extreme goodness, whose self-denial approaches to heroism, and who devote themselves in obscurity to a life of martyrdom - pure and heavenly minds, in whom the instincts of the heart supply the place of the intellect!

The only defect, or rather the necessary consequence of this extreme simplicity of character, was the invincible determination she displayed in yielding to the commands of her confessor, to whose influence she had now for many years been accustomed to submit. She regarded this influence as most venerable and sacred; no mortal power, no human consideration, could have prevented her from obeying it. Did any dispute arise on the subject, nothing could move her on this point; she opposed to every argument a resistance entirely free from passion - mild as her disposition, calm as her conscience - but, like the latter, not to be shaken. In a word, Frances Baudoin was one of those pure, but uninstructed and credulous beings, who may sometimes, in skillful and dangerous hands, become, without knowing it, the instruments of much evil.

For some time past, the bad state of her health, and particularly the increasing weakness of her sight, had condemned her to a forced repose; unable to work more than two or three hours a day, she consumed the rest of her time at church.

Frances rose from her seat, pushed the coarse bags at which she had been working to the further end of the table, and proceeded to lay the cloth for her son's supper, with maternal care and solicitude. She took from the press a small leathern bag, containing an old silver cup, very much battered, and a fork and spoon, so worn and thin, that the latter cut like a knife. These, her only plate (the wedding present of Dagobert) she rubbed and polished as well as she was able, and laid by the side of her son's plate. They were the most precious of her possessions, not so much for what little intrinsic value might attach to them, as for the associations they recalled; and she had often shed bitter tears, when, under the pressure of illness or want of employment, she had been compelled to carry these sacred treasures to the pawnbroker's.

Frances next took, from the lower shelf of the press, a bottle of water, and one of wine about three-quarters full, which she also placed near her son's plate; she then returned to the stove, to watch the cooking of the supper.

Though Agricola was not much later than usual, the countenance of his mother expressed both uneasiness and grief; one might have seen, by the redness of her eyes, that she had been weeping a good deal. After long and painful uncertainty, the poor woman had just arrived at the conviction that her eyesight, which had been growing weaker and weaker, would soon be so much impaired as to prevent her working even the two or three hours a day which had lately been the extent of her labors.

Originally an excellent hand at her needle, she had been obliged, as her eyesight gradually failed her, to abandon the finer for the coarser sorts of work, and her earnings had necessarily diminished in proportion; she had at length been reduced to the necessity of making those coarse bags for the army, which took about four yards of sewing, and were paid at the rate of two sous each, she having to find her own thread. This work, being very hard, she could at most complete three such bags in a day, and her gains thus amounted to threepence (six sous)!

It makes one shudder to think of the great number of unhappy females, whose strength has been so much exhausted by privations, old age, or sickness, that all the labor of which they are capable, hardly suffices to bring them in daily this miserable pittance. Thus do their gains diminish in exact proportion to the increasing wants which age and infirmity must occasion.

Happily, Frances had an efficient support in her son. A first-rate workman, profiting by the just scale of wages adopted by M. Hardy, his labor brought him from four to five shillings a day - more than double what was gained by the workmen of many other establishments. Admitting therefore that his mother were to gain nothing, he could easily maintain both her and himself.

But the poor woman, so wonderfully economical that she denied herself even some of the necessaries of life, had of late become ruinously liberal on the score of the sacristy, since she had adopted the habit of visiting daily the parish church. Scarcely a day passed but she had masses sung, or tapers burnt, either for Dagobert, from whom she had been so long separated, or for the salvation of her son Agricola, whom she considered on the high-road to perdition. Agricola had so excellent a heart, so loved and revered his mother, and considered her actions in this respect inspired by so touching a sentiment, that he never complained when he saw a great part of his week's wages (which he paid regularly over to his mother every Saturday) disappear in pious forms.

Yet now and then he ventured to remark to Frances, with as much respect as tenderness, that it pained him to see her enduring privations injurious at her age, because she preferred incurring these devotional expenses. But what answer could he make to this excellent mother, when she replied with tears: "My child, 'tis for the salvation of your father and yours too."

To dispute the efficacy of masses, would have been venturing on a subject which Agricola, through respect for his mother's religious faith, never discussed. He contented himself, therefore, with seeing her dispense with comforts she might have enjoyed.

A discreet tap was heard at the door. "Come in," said Frances. The person came in.

CHAPTER XXVIII

THE SISTER OF THE BACCHANAL QUEEN

The person who now entered was a girl of about eighteen, short, and very much deformed. Though not exactly a hunchback, her spine was curved; her breast was sunken, and her head deeply set in the shoulders. Her face was regular, but long, thin, very pale, and pitted with the small pox; yet it expressed great sweetness and melancholy. Her blue eyes beamed with kindness and intelligence. By a strange freak of nature, the handsomest woman would have been proud of the magnificent hair twisted in a coarse net at the back of her head. She held an old basket in her hand. Though miserably clad, the care and neatness of her dress revealed a powerful struggle with her poverty. Notwithstanding the cold, she wore a scanty frock made of print of an indefinable color, spotted with white; but it had been so often washed, that its primitive design and color had long since disappeared. In her resigned, yet suffering face, might be read a long familiarity with every form of suffering, every description of taunting. From her birth, ridicule had ever pursued her. We have said that she was very deformed, and she was vulgarly called "Mother Bunch." Indeed it was so usual to give her this grotesque name, which every moment reminded her of her infirmity, that Frances and Agricola, though they felt as much compassion as other people showed contempt for her, never called her, however, by any other name.

Mother Bunch, as we shall therefore call her in future, was

born in the house in which Dagobert's wife had resided for more than twenty years; and she had, as it were, been brought up with Agricola and Gabriel.

There are wretches fatally doomed to misery. Mother Bunch had a very pretty sister, on whom Perrine Soliveau, their common mother, the widow of a ruined tradesman, had concentrated all her affection, while she treated her deformed child with contempt and unkindness. The latter would often come, weeping, to Frances, on this account, who tried to console her, and in the long evenings amused her by teaching her to read and sew. Accustomed to pity her by their mother's example, instead of imitating other children, who always taunted and sometimes even beat her, Agricola and Gabriel liked her, and used to protect and defend her.

She was about fifteen, and her sister Cephyse was about seventeen, when their mother died, leaving them both in utter poverty. Cephyse was intelligent, active, clever, but different to her sister; she had the lively, alert, hoydenish character which requires air, exercise and pleasures - a good girl enough, but foolishly spoiled by her mother. Cephyse, listening at first to Frances's good advice, resigned herself to her lot; and, having learnt to sew, worked like her sister, for about a year. But, unable to endure any longer the bitter privations her insignificant earnings, notwithstanding her incessant toil, exposed her to - privations which often bordered on starvation - Cephyse, young, pretty, of warm temperament, and surrounded by brilliant offers and seductions - brilliant, indeed, for her, since they offered food to satisfy her hunger, shelter from the cold, and decent raiment, without being obliged to work fifteen hours a day in an obscure and unwholesome hovel - Cephyse listened to the vows of a young lawyer's clerk, who forsook her soon after. She formed a connection with another clerk, whom she (instructed by the examples set her), forsook in turn for a bagman, whom she afterwards cast off for other favorites. In a word, what with changing and being forsaken, Cephyse, in the course of one or two years, was the idol of a set of grisettes, students and clerks;

and acquired such a reputation at the balls on the Hampstead Heaths of Paris, by her decision of character, original turn of mind, and unwearied ardor in all kinds of pleasures, and especially her wild, noisy gayety, that she was termed the Bacchanal Queen, and proved herself in every way worthy of this bewildering royalty.

From that time poor Mother Bunch only heard of her sister at rare intervals. She still mourned for her, and continued to toil hard to gain her three-and-six a week. The unfortunate girl, having been taught sewing by Frances, made coarse shirts for the common people and the army. For these she received half-a-crown a dozen. They had to be hemmed, stitched, provided with collars and wristbands, buttons, and button holes; and at the most, when at work twelve and fifteen hours a day, she rarely succeeded in turning out more than fourteen or sixteen shirts a week - an excessive amount of toil that brought her in about three shillings and fourpence a week. And the case of this poor girl was neither accidental nor uncommon. And this, because the remuneration given for women's work is an example of revolting injustice and savage barbarism. They are paid not half as much as men who are employed at the needle: such as tailors, and makers of gloves, or waistcoats, etc. - no doubt because women can work as well as men - because they are more weak and delicate - and because their need may be twofold as great when they become mothers.

Well, Mother Bunch fagged on, with three-and-four a week. That is to say, toiling hard for twelve or fifteen hours every day; she succeeded in keeping herself alive, in spite of exposure to hunger, cold, and poverty - so numerous were her privations. Privations? No! The word privation expresses but weakly that constant and terrible want of all that is necessary to preserve the existence God gives; namely, wholesome air and shelter, sufficient and nourishing food and warm clothing. Mortification would be a better word to describe that total want of all that is essentially vital, which a justly organized state of society ought - yes - ought necessarily to bestow on every active, honest workman and workwoman, since civilization has dispossessed them of all territorial right, and left them no other patrimony than their hands.

The savage does not enjoy the advantage of civilization; but he has, at least, the beasts of the field, the fowls of the air, the fish of the sea, and the fruits of the earth, to feed him, and his native woods for shelter and for fuel. The civilized man, disinherited of these gifts, considering the rights of property as sacred, may, in return for his hard daily labor, which enriches his country, demand wages that will enable him to live in the enjoyment of health: nothing more, and nothing less. For is it living, to drag along on the extreme edge which separates life from the grave, and even there continually struggle against cold, hunger, and disease? And to show how far the mortification which society imposes thus inexorably on its millions of honest, industrious laborers (by its careless disregard of all the questions which concern the just remuneration of labor), may extend, we will describe how this poor girl contrived to live on three shillings and sixpence a week.

Society, perhaps, may then feel its obligation to so many unfortunate wretches for supporting, with resignation, the horrible existence which leaves them just sufficient life to feel the worst pangs of humanity. Yes: to live at such a price is virtue! Yes, society thus organized, whether it tolerates or imposes so much misery, loses all right to blame the poor wretches who sell themselves not through debauchery, but because they are cold and famishing. This poor girl spent her wages as follows:

Six pounds of bread, second quality	8 1/2
Four pails of water	0 2
Lard or dripping (butter being out of the question)	0 5
Coarse salt	0 3/4
A bushel of charcoal	0 4
A quart of dried vegetables	0 3
Three quarts of potatoes	0 2
Dips	0 3 1/4
Thread and needles	0 2 1/2

To save charcoal, Mother Bunch prepared soup only two or three times a week at most, on a stove that stood on the landing of the fourth story. On other days she ate it cold. There remained nine or ten pence a week for clothes and lodging. By rare good fortune, her situation was in one respect an exception to the lot of many others. Agricola, that he might not wound her delicacy, had come to a secret arrangement with the housekeeper, and hired a garret for her, just large enough to hold a small bed, a chair, and a table; for which the sempstress had to pay five shillings a year. But Agricola, in fulfilment of his agreement with the porter, paid the balance, to make up the actual rent of the garret, which was twelve and sixpence. The poor girl had thus about eighteenpence a month left for her other expenses. But many workwomen, whose position is less fortunate than hers, since they have neither home nor family, buy a piece of bread and some other food to keep them through the day; and at night patronize the "twopenny rope," one with another, in a wretched room containing five or six beds, some of which are always engaged by men, as male lodgers are by far the most abundant. Yes; and in spite of the disgust that a poor and virtuous girl must feel at this arrangement, she must submit to it; for a lodging-house keeper cannot have separate rooms for females. To furnish a room, however meanly, the poor workwoman must possess three or four shillings in ready money. But how save this sum, out of weekly earnings of a couple of florins, which are scarcely sufficient to keep her from starving, and are still less sufficient to clothe her? No! no! The poor wretch must resign herself to this repugnant cohabitation; and so, gradually, the instinct of modesty becomes weakened; the natural sentiment of chastity, that saved her from the "gay life," becomes extinct; vice appears to be the only means of improving her intolerable condition; she yields; and the first "man made of money," who can afford a governess for his children, cries out against the depravity of the lower orders! And yet, painful as the condition of the working woman is, it is relatively fortunate. Should work fail her for one day, two days, what then? Should sickness come - sickness almost always occasioned by unwholesome food, want of fresh air, necessary attention, and good rest; sickness, often so enervating as to render work impossible; though not so dangerous as to procure the sufferer a bed in an hospital - what becomes of the hapless wretches then? The mind hesitates, and shrinks from dwelling on such gloomy pictures.

This inadequacy of wages, one terrible source only of so many evils, and often of so many vices, is general, especially among women; and, again this is not private wretchedness, but the wretchedness which afflicts whole classes, the type of which we endeavor to develop in Mother Bunch. It exhibits the moral and physical condition of thousands of human creatures in Paris, obliged to subsist on a scanty four shillings a week. This poor workwoman, then, notwithstanding the advantages she unknowingly enjoyed through Agricola's generosity, lived very miserably; and her health, already shattered, was now wholly undermined by these constant hardships. Yet, with extreme delicacy, though ignorant of the little sacrifice already made for her by Agricola, Mother Bunch pretended she earned more than she really did, in order to avoid offers of service which it would have pained her to accept, because she knew the limited means of Frances and her son, and because it would have wounded her natural delicacy, rendered still more sensitive by so many sorrows and humiliations.

But, singular as it may appear, this deformed body contained a loving and generous soul - a mind cultivated even to poetry; and let us add, that this was owing to the example of Agricola Baudoin, with whom she had been brought up, and who had naturally the gift. This poor girl was the first confidant to whom our young mechanic imparted his literary essays; and when he told her of the charm and extreme relief he found in poetic reverie, after a day of hard toil, the workwoman, gifted with strong natural intelligence, felt, in her turn, how great a resource this would be to her in her lonely and despised condition.

One day, to Agricola's great surprise, who had just read some verses to her, the sewing-girl, with smiles and blushes, timidly communicated to him also a poetic composition. Her verses wanted rhythm and harmony, perhaps; but they were simple and affecting, as a non-envenomed complaint entrusted to a friendly hearer. From that day Agricola and she held frequent consultations; they gave each other mutual encouragement: but with this exception, no one else knew anything of the girl's poetical essays, whose mild timidity made her often pass for a person of weak intellect. This soul must have been great and beautiful, for in all her unlettered strains there was not a word of murmuring respecting her hard lot: her note was sad, but gentle - desponding, but resigned; it was especially the language of deep tenderness - of mournful sympathy - of angelic charity for all poor creatures consigned, like her, to bear the double burden of poverty and deformity. Yet she often expressed a sincere free-spoken admiration of beauty, free from all envy or bitterness; she admired beauty as she admired the sun. But, alas! many were the verses of hers that Agricola had never seen, and which he was never to see.

The young mechanic, though not strictly handsome, had an open masculine face; was as courageous as kind; possessed a noble, glowing, generous heart, a superior mind, and a frank, pleasing gayety of spirits. The young girl, brought up with him, loved him as an unfortunate creature can love, who, dreading cruel ridicule, is obliged to hide her affection in the depths of her heart, and adopt reserve and deep dissimulation. She did not seek to combat her love; to what purpose should she do so? No one would ever know it. Her well known sisterly affection for Agricola explained the interest she took in all that concerned him; so that no one was surprised at the extreme grief of the young workwoman, when, in 1830, Agricola, after fighting intrepidly for the people's flag, was brought bleeding home to his mother. Dagobert's son, deceived, like others, on this point, had never suspected, and was destined never to suspect, this love for him.

Such was the poorly-clad girl who entered the room in which

Frances was preparing her son's supper.

"Is it you, my poor love," said she; "I have not seen you since morning: have you been ill? Come and kiss me."

The young girl kissed Agricola's mother, and replied: "I was very busy about some work, mother; I did not wish to lose a moment; I have only just finished it. I am going down to fetch some charcoal - do you want anything while I'm out?"

"No, no, my child, thank you. But I am very uneasy. It is half-past eight, and Agricola is not come home." Then she added, after a sigh: "He kills himself with work for me. Ah, I am very unhappy, my girl; my sight is quite going. In a quarter of an hour after I begin working, I cannot see at all - not even to sew sacks. The idea of being a burden to my son drives me distracted."

"Oh, don't, ma'am, if Agricola heard you say that -"

"I know the poor boy thinks of nothing but me, and that augments my vexation. Only I think that rather than leave me, he gives up the advantages that his fellow-workmen enjoy at Hardy's, his good and worthy master - instead of living in this dull garret, where it is scarcely light at noon, he would enjoy, like the other workmen, at very little expense, a good light room, warm in winter, airy in summer, with a view of the garden. And he is so fond of trees! not to mention that this place is so far from his work, that it is quite a toil to him to get to it."

"Oh, when he embraces you he forgets his fatigue, Mrs. Baudoin," said Mother Bunch; "besides, he knows how you cling to the house in which he was born. M. Hardy offered to settle you at Plessy with Agricola, in the building put up for the workmen."

"Yes, my child; but then I must give up church. I can't do that."

"But - be easy, I hear him," said the hunchback, blushing.

A sonorous, joyous voice was heard singing on the stairs.

"At least, I'll not let him see that I have been crying," said the good mother, drying her tears. "This is the only moment of rest and ease from toil he has - I must not make it sad to him."

CHAPTER XXIX

AGRICOLA BAUDOIN

Our blacksmith poet, a tall young man, about four-and-twenty years of age, was alert and robust, with ruddy complexion, dark hair and eyes, and aquiline nose, and an open, expressive countenance. His resemblance to Dagobert was rendered more striking by the thick brown moustache which he wore according to the fashion; and a sharp-pointed imperial covered his chin. His cheeks, however, were shaven, Olive color velveteen trousers, a blue blouse, bronzed by the forge smoke, a black cravat, tied carelessly round his muscular neck, a cloth cap with a narrow vizor, composed his dress. The only thing which contrasted singularly with his working habiliments was a handsome purple flower, with silvery pistils, which he held in his hand.

"Good-evening, mother," said he, as he came to kiss Frances immediately.

Then, with a friendly nod, he added, "Good-evening, Mother Bunch."

"You are very late, my child," said Frances, approaching the little stove on which her son's simple meal was simmering; "I was getting very anxious."

"Anxious about me, or about my supper, dear mother?" said Agricola, gayly. "The deuce! you won't excuse me for keeping the nice little supper waiting that you get ready for me, for fear it should be spoilt, eh?"

So saying, the blacksmith tried to kiss his mother again.

"Have done, you naughty boy; you'll make me upset the pan."

"That would be a pity, mother; for it smells delightfully. Let's see what it is."

"Wait half a moment."

"I'll swear, now, you have some of the fried potatoes and bacon I'm so fond of."

"Being Saturday, of course!" said Frances, in a tone of mild reproach.

"True," rejoined Agricola, exchanging a smile of innocent cunning with Mother Bunch; "but, talking of Saturday, mother, here are my wages."

"Thank ye, child; put the money in the cupboard."

"Yes, mother!"

"Oh, dear!" cried the young sempstress, just as Agricola was about to put away the money, "what a handsome flower you have in your hand, Agricola. I never saw a finer. In winter, too! Do look at it, Mrs. Baudoin."

"See there, mother," said Agricola, taking the flower to her; "look at it, admire it, and especially smell it. You can't have a sweeter perfume; a blending of vanilla and orange blossom."

"Indeed, it does smell nice, child. Goodness! how handsome!" said Frances, admiringly; "where did you find it?"

"Find it, my good mother!" repeated Agricola, smilingly: "do you think folks pick up such things between the Barriere du Maine and the Rue Brise-Miche?"

"How did you get it then?" inquired the sewing girl, sharing in Frances's curiosity.

"Oh! you would like to know? Well, I'll satisfy you, and explain why I came home so late; for something else detained me. It has been an evening of adventures, I promise you. I was hurrying home, when I heard a low, gentle barking at the corner of the Rue de Babylone; it was just about dusk, and I could see a very pretty little dog, scarce bigger than my fist, black and tan, with long, silky hair, and ears that covered its paws."

"Lost, poor thing, I warrant," said Frances.

"You've hit it. I took up the poor thing, and it began to lick my hands. Round its neck was a red satin ribbon, tied in a large bow; but as that did not bear the master's name, I looked beneath it, and saw a small collar, made of a gold plate and small gold chains. So I took a Lucifer match from my 'bacco-box, and striking a light, I read, 'FRISKY belongs to Hon. Miss Adrienne de Cardoville, No. 7, Rue de Babylone.'"

"Why, you were just in the street," said Mother Bunch.

"Just so. Taking the little animal under my arm, I looked about me till I came to a long garden wall, which seemed to have no end, and found a small door of a summer-house, belonging no doubt to the large mansion at the other end of the park; for this garden looked just like a park. So, looking up I saw 'No. 7,' newly painted over a little door with a grated slide. I rang; and in a few minutes, spent, no doubt, in observing me through the bars (for I am sure I saw a pair of eyes peeping through), the gate opened. And now, you'll not believe a word I have to say."

"Why not, my child?"

"Because it seems like a fairy tale."

"A fairy tale?" said Mother Bunch, as if she was really her namesake of elfish history.

"For, all the world it does. I am quite astounded, even now, at my adventure; it is like the remembrance of a dream."

"Well, let us have it," said the worthy mother, so deeply interested that she did not perceive her son's supper was beginning to burn.

"First," said the blacksmith, smiling at the curiosity he had excited, "a young lady opened the door to me, but so lovely, so beautifully and gracefully dressed, that you would have taken her for a beautiful portrait of past times. Before I could say a word, she exclaimed, 'Ah! dear me, sir, you have brought back Frisky; how happy Miss Adrienne will be! Come, pray come in instantly; she would so regret not having an opportunity to thank you in person!' And without giving me time to reply, she beckoned me to follow her. Oh, dear mother, it is quite out of my power to tell you, the magnificence I saw, as I passed through a small saloon, partially lighted, and full of perfume! It would be impossible. The young woman walked too quickly. A door opened, - Oh, such a sight! I was so dazzled I can remember nothing but a great glare of gold and light, crystal and flowers; and, amidst all this brilliancy, a young lady of extreme beauty - ideal beauty; but she had red hair, or rather hair shining like gold! Oh! it was charming to look at! I never saw such hair before. She had black eyes, ruddy lips, and her skin seemed white as snow. This is all I can recollect: for, as I said before, I was so dazzled, I seemed to be looking through a veil. 'Madame,' said the young woman, whom I never should have taken for a lady's-maid, she was dressed so elegantly, 'here is Frisky. This gentleman found him, and brought him back.' 'Oh, sir,' said the young lady with the golden hair, in a sweet silvery voice, 'what thanks I owe you! I am foolishly attached to Frisky.' Then, no doubt, concluding from my dress that she ought to thank me in some other way than by words, she took up a silk purse, and said to me, though I must confess with some hesitation - 'No doubt, sir, it gave you some trouble to bring my pet back. You have, perhaps, lost some valuable time - allow me -' She held forth her purse."

"Oh, Agricola," said Mother Bunch, sadly; "how people may be deceived!"

"Hear the end, and you will perhaps forgive the young lady. Seeing by my looks that the offer of the purse hurt me, she took a magnificent porcelain vase that contained this flower, and, addressing me in a tone full of grace and kindness, that left me room to guess that she was vexed at having wounded me, she said - 'At least, sir, you will accept this flower.'"

"You are right, Agricola," said the girl, smiling sadly; "an involuntary error could not be repaired in a nicer way.

"Worthy young lady," said Frances, wiping her eyes; "how well she understood my Agricola!"

"Did she not, mother? But just as I was taking the flower, without daring to raise my eyes (for, notwithstanding the young lady's kind manner, there was something very imposing about her) another handsome girl, tall and dark, and dressed to the top of fashion, came in and said to the red-haired young lady, 'He is here, Madame.' She immediately rose and said to me, 'A thousand pardons, sir. I shall never forget that I am indebted to you for a moment of much pleasure. Pray remember, on all occasions, my address and name - Adrienne de Cardoville.' Thereupon she disappeared. I could not find a word to say in reply. The same young woman showed me to the door, and curtseyed to me very politely. And there I stood in the Rue de Babylone, as dazzled and astonished as if I had come out of an enchanted palace."

"Indeed, my child, it is like a fairy tale. Is it not, my poor girl?"

"Yes, ma'am," said Mother Bunch, in an absent manner that

Agricola did not observe.

"What affected me most," rejoined Agricola, "was, that the young lady, on seeing her little dog, did not forget me for it, as many would have done in her place, and took no notice of it before me. That shows delicacy and feeling, does it not? Indeed, I believe this young lady to be so kind and generous, that I should not hesitate to have recourse to her in any important case."

"Yes, you are right," replied the sempstress, more and more absent.

The poor girl suffered extremely. She felt no jealousy, no hatred, towards this young stranger, who, from her beauty, wealth, and delicacy, seemed to belong to a sphere too splendid and elevated to be even within the reach of a work, girl's vision; but, making an involuntary comparison of this fortunate condition with her own, the poor thing had never felt more cruelly her deformity and poverty. Yet such were the humility and gentle resignation of this noble creature, that the only thing which made her feel ill-disposed towards Adrienne de Cardoville was the offer of the purse to Agricola; but then the charming way in which the young lady had atoned for her error, affected the sempstress deeply. Yet her heart was ready to break. She could not restrain her tears as she contemplated the magnificent flower - so rich in color and perfume, which, given by a charming hand, was doubtless very precious to Agricola.

"Now, mother," resumed the young man smilingly, and unaware of the painful emotion of the other bystander, "you have had the cream of my adventures first. I have told you one of the causes of my delay; and now for the other. Just now, as I was coming in, I met the dyer at the foot of the stairs, his arms a beautiful pea-green. Stopping me he said, with an air full of importance, that he thought he had seen a chap sneaking about the house like a spy, 'Well, what is that to you, Daddy Loriot?' said I: 'are you afraid he will nose out the way to make the beautiful green, with which you are dyed up to the very elbows?'"

"But who could that man be, Agricola?" said Frances.

"On my word, mother, I don't know and scarcely care; I tried to persuade Daddy Loriot, who chatters like a magpie, to return to his cellar, since it could signify as little to him as to me, whether a spy watched him or not." So saying, Agricola went and placed the little leathern sack, containing his wages, on a shelf, in the cupboard.

As Frances put down the saucepan on the end of the table, Mother Bunch, recovering from her reverie, filled a basin with water, and, taking it to the blacksmith, said to him in a gentle tone-"Agricola - for your hands."

"Thank you, little sister. How kind you are!" Then with a most unaffected gesture and tone, he added, "There is my fine flower for your trouble."

"Do you give it me?" cried the sempstress, with emotion, while a vivid blush colored her pale and interesting face. "Do you give me this handsome flower, which a lovely rich young lady so kindly and graciously gave you?" And the poor thing repeated, with growing astonishment, "Do you give it to me?"

"What the deuce should I do with it? Wear it on my heart, have it set as a pin?" said Agricola, smiling. "It is true I was very much impressed by the charming way in which the young lady thanked me. I am delighted to think I found her little dog, and very happy to be able to give you this flower, since it pleases you. You see the day has been a happy one."

While Mother Bunch, trembling with pleasure, emotion, and surprise, took the flower, the young blacksmith washed his hands, so black with smoke and steel filings that the water became dark in an instant. Agricola, pointing out this change to the sempstress, said to her in a whisper, laughing,-"Here's cheap ink for us paper-stainers! I finished some verses yesterday, which I am rather satisfied with. I will read them to you."

With this, Agricola wiped his hands naturally on the front of his blouse, while Mother Bunch replaced the basin on the chest of drawers, and laid the flower against the side of it.

"Can't you ask for a towel," said Frances, shrugging her shoulders, "instead of wiping your hands on your blouse?"

"After being scorched all day long at the forge, it will be all the better for a little cooling to-night, won't it? Am I disobedient, mother? Scold me, then, if you dare! Come, let us see you."

Frances made no reply; but, placing her hands on either side of her son's head, so beautiful in its candor, resolution and intelligence, she surveyed him for a moment with maternal pride, and kissed him repeatedly on the forehead.

"Come," said she, "sit down: you stand all day at your forge, and it is late."

"So, - your arm-chair again!" said Agricola. - "Our usual quarrel every evening - take it away, I shall be quite as much at ease on another."

"No, no! You ought at least to rest after your hard toil."

"What tyranny!" said Agricola gayly, sitting down. "Well, I preach like a good apostle; but I am quite at ease in your arm-chair, after all. Since I sat down on the throne in the Tuileries, I have never had a better seat."

Frances Baudoin, standing on one side of the table, cut a slice of bread for her son, while Mother Bunch, on the other, filled his silver mug. There was something affecting in the attentive eagerness of the two excellent creatures, for him whom they loved so tenderly.

"Won't you sup with me?" said Agricola to the girl.

"Thank you, Agricola," replied the sempstress, looking down, "I have only just dined."

"Oh, I only ask you for form's sake - you have your whims - we can never prevail on you to eat with us - just like mother; she prefers dining all alone; and in that way she deprives herself without my knowing it."

"Goodness, child! It is better for my health to dine early. Well, do you find it nice?"

"Nice! - call it excellent! Stockfish and parsnips. Oh, I am very fond of stockfish; I should have been born a Newfoundland fisherman."

This worthy lad, on the contrary, was but poorly refreshed, after a hard day's toil, with this paltry stew, - a little burnt as it had been, too, during his story; but he knew he pleased his mother by observing the fast without complaining. He affected to enjoy his meal; and the good woman accordingly observed with satisfaction:

"Oh, I see you like it, my dear boy; Friday and Saturday next we'll have some more."

"Thank you, mother, - only not two days together. One gets tired of luxuries, you know! And now, let us talk of what we shall do to-morrow - Sunday. We must be very merry, for the last few days you seem very sad, dear mother, and I can't make it out - I fancy you are not satisfied with me."

"Oh, my dear child! - you - the pattern of -"

"Well, well! Prove to me that you are happy, then, by taking a little amusement. Perhaps you will do us the honor of accompanying us, as you did last time," added Agricola, bowing to Mother Bunch.

The latter blushed and looked down; her face assumed an expression of bitter grief, and she made no reply.

"I have the prayers to attend all day, you know, my dear child," said Frances to her son.

"Well, in the evening, then? I don't propose the theatre; but they say there is a conjurer to be seen whose tricks are very amusing.

"I am obliged to you, my son; but that is a kind of theatre."

"Dear mother, this is unreasonable!"

"My dear child, do I ever hinder others from doing what they like?"

"True, dear mother; forgive me. Well, then, if it should be fine, we will simply take a walk with Mother Bunch on the Boulevards. It is nearly three months since she went out with us; and she never goes out without us."

"No, no; go alone, my child. Enjoy your Sunday, 'tis little enough."

"You know very well, Agricola," said the sempstress, blushing up to the eyes, "that I ought not to go out with you and your mother again."

"Why not, madame? May I ask, without impropriety, the cause of this refusal?" said Agricola gayly.

The poor girl smiled sadly, and replied, "Because I will not expose you to a quarrel on my account, Agricola."

"Forgive me," said Agricola, in a tone of sincere grief, and he struck his forehead vexedly.

To this Mother Bunch alluded sometimes, but very rarely, for she observed punctilious discretion. The girl had gone out with Agricola and his mother. Such occasions were, indeed, holidays for her. Many days and nights had she toiled hard to procure a decent bonnet and shawl, that she might not do discredit to her friends. The five or six days of holidays, thus spent arm in arm with him whom she adored in secret, formed the sum of her happy days.

Taking their last walk, a coarse, vulgar man elbowed her so rudely that the poor girl could not refrain from a cry of terror, and the man retorted it by saying,-"What are you rolling your hump in my way for, stoopid?"

Agricola, like his father, had the patience which force and courage give to the truly brave; but he was extremely quick when it became necessary to avenge an insult. Irritated at the vulgarity of this man, Agricola left his mother's arm to inflict on the brute, who was of his own age, size, and force, two vigorous blows, such as the powerful arm and huge fist of a blacksmith never before inflicted on human face. The villain attempted to return it, and Agricola repeated the correction, to the amusement of the crowd, and the fellow slunk away amidst a deluge of hisses. This adventure made Mother Bunch say she would not go out with Agricola again, in order to save him any occasion of quarrel. We may conceive the blacksmith's regret at having thus unwittingly revived the memory of this circumstance, - more painful, alas! for Mother Bunch than Agricola could imagine, for she loved him passionately, and her infirmity had been the cause of that quarrel. Notwithstanding his strength and resolution, Agricola was childishly sensitive; and, thinking how painful that thought must be to the poor girl, a large tear filled his eyes, and, holding out his hands, he said, in a brotherly tone, "Forgive my heedlessness! Come, kiss me." And he gave her thin, pale cheeks two hearty kisses.

The poor girl's lips turned pale at this cordial caress; and her heart beat so violently that she was obliged to lean against the corner of the table.

"Come, you forgive me, do you not?" said Agricola.

"Yes! yes!" she said, trying to subdue her emotion; "but the recollection of that quarrel pains me - I was so alarmed on your account; if the crowd had sided with that man!"

"Alas!" said Frances, coming to the sewing-girl's relief, without knowing it, "I was never so afraid in all my life!"

"Oh, mother," rejoined Agricola, trying to change a conversation which had now become disagreeable for the sempstress, "for the wife of a horse grenadier of the Imperial Guard, you have not much courage. Oh, my brave father; I can't believe he is really coming! The very thought turns me topsy-turvy!"

"Heaven grant he may come," said Frances, with a sigh.

"God grant it, mother. He will grant it, I should think. Lord knows, you have had masses enough said for his return."

"Agricola, my child," said Frances, interrupting her son, and shaking her head sadly, "do not speak in that way. Besides, you are talking of your father."

"Well, I'm in for it this evening. 'Tis your turn now; positively, I am growing stupid, or going crazy. Forgive me, mother! forgive! That's the only word I can get out to-night. You know that, when I do let out on certain subjects, it is because I can't help it; for I know well the pain it gives you."

"You do not offend me, my poor, dear, misguided boy."

"It comes to the same thing; and there is nothing so bad as to offend one's mother; and, with respect to what I said about father's return, I do not see that we have any cause to doubt it."

"But we have not heard from him for four months."

"You know, mother, in his letter - that is, in the letter which he dictated (for you remember that, with the candor of an old soldier, he told us that, if he could read tolerably well, he could not write); well, in that letter he said we were not to be anxious about him; that he expected to be in Paris about the end of January, and would send us word, three or four days before, by what road he expected to arrive, that I might go and meet him."

"True, my child; and February is come, and no news yet."

"The greater reason why we should wait patiently. But I'll tell you more: I should not be surprised if our good Gabriel were to come back about the same time. His last letter from America makes me hope so. What pleasure, mother, should all the family be together!"

"Oh, yes, my child! It would be a happy day for me."

"And that day will soon come, trust me."

"Do you remember your father, Agricola?" inquired Mother Bunch.

"To tell the truth, I remember most his great grenadier's shako and moustache, which used to frighten me so, that nothing but the red ribbon of his cross of honor, on the white facings of his uniform, and the shining handle of his sabre, could pacify me; could it, mother? But what is the matter? You are weeping!"

"Alas! poor Baudoin! What he must suffer at being separated from us at his age - sixty and past! Alas! my child, my heart breaks, when I think that he comes home only to change one kind of poverty for another."

"What do you mean?"

"Alas! I earn nothing now."

"Why, what's become of me? Isn't there a room here for you and for him; and a table for you too? Only, my good mother, since we are talking of domestic affairs," added the blacksmith, imparting increased tenderness to his tone, that he might not shock his mother, "when he and Gabriel come home, you won't want to have any more masses said, and tapers burned for them, will you? Well, that saving will enable father to have tobacco to smoke, and his bottle of wine every day. Then, on Sundays, we will take a nice dinner at the eating-house."

A knocking at the door disturbed Agricola.

"Come in," said he. Instead of doing so, some one half-opened the door, and, thrusting in an arm of a pea-green color, made signs to the blacksmith.

"'Tis old Loriot, the pattern of dyers," said Agricola; "come in, Daddy, no ceremony."

"Impossible, my lad; I am dripping with dye from head to foot; I should cover missus's floor with green."

"So much the better. It will remind me of the fields I like so much."

"Without joking, Agricola, I must speak to you immediately."

"About the spy, eh? Oh, be easy; what's he to us?"

"No; I think he's gone; at any rate, the fog is so thick I can't see him. But that's not it - come, come quickly! It is very important," said the dyer, with a mysterious look; "and only concerns you."

"Me, only?" said Agricola, with surprise. "What can it be.

"Go and see, my child," said Frances.

"Yes, mother; but the deuce take me if I can make it out."

And the blacksmith left the room, leaving his mother with Mother Bunch.

CHAPTER XXX

THE RETURN

In five minutes Agricola returned; his face was pale and agitated - his eyes glistened with tears, and his hands trembled; but his countenance expressed extraordinary happiness and emotion. He stood at the door for a moment, as if too much affected to accost his mother.

Frances's sight was so bad that she did not immediately perceive the change her son's countenance had undergone.

"Well, my child - what is it?" she inquired.

Before the blacksmith could reply, Mother Bunch, who had more discernment, exclaimed: "Goodness, Agricola - how pale you are! Whatever is the matter?"

"Mother," said the artisan, hastening to Frances, without replying to the sempstress, - "mother, expect news that will astonish you; but promise me you will be calm."

"What do you mean? How you tremble! Look at me! Mother Bunch was right - you are quite pale."

"My kind mother!" and Agricola, kneeling before Frances, took both her hands in his - "you must - you do not know, - but -"

The blacksmith could not go on. Tears of joy interrupted his speech.

"You weep, my dear child! Your tears alarm me. 'What is the matter? - you terrify me!"

"Oh, no, I would not terrify you; on the contrary," said Agricola, drying his eyes - "you will be so happy. But, again, you must try and command your feelings, for too much joy is as hurtful as too much grief."

"What?"

"Did I not say true, when I said he would come?"

"Father!" cried Frances. She rose from her seat; but her surprise and emotion were so great that she put one hand to her heart to still its beating, and then she felt her strength fail. Her son sustained her, and assisted her to sit down.

Mother Bunch, till now, had stood discreetly apart, witnessing from a distance the scene which completely engrossed Agricola and his mother. But she now drew near timidly, thinking she might be useful; for Frances changed color more and more.

"Come, courage, mother," said the blacksmith; "now the shock is over, you have only to enjoy the pleasure of seeing my father."

"My poor man! after eighteen years' absence. Oh, I cannot believe it," said Frances, bursting into tears. "Is it true? Is it, indeed, true?"

"So true, that if you will promise me to keep as calm as you can, I will tell you when you may see him."

"Soon - may I not?"

"Yes; soon."

"But when will he arrive?"

"He may arrive any minute - to-morrow - perhaps to-day."

"To-day!"

"Yes, mother! Well, I must tell you all - he has arrived."

"He - he is -" Frances could not articulate the word.

"He was downstairs just now. Before coming up, he sent the dyer to apprise me that I might prepare you; for my brave father feared the surprise might hurt you."

"Oh, heaven!"

"And now," cried the blacksmith, in an accent of indescribable joy - "he is there, waiting! Oh, mother! for the last ten minutes I have scarcely been able to contain myself - my heart is bursting with joy." And running to the door, he threw it open.

Dagobert, holding Rose and Blanche by the hand, stood on the threshold. Instead of rushing to her husband's arms, Frances fell on her knees in prayer. She thanked heaven with profound gratitude for hearing her prayers, and thus accepting her offerings. During a second, the actors of this scene stood silent and motionless. Agricola, by a sentiment of respect and delicacy, which struggled violently with his affection, did not dare to fall on his father's neck. He waited with constrained impatience till his mother had finished her prayer.

The soldier experienced the same feeling as the blacksmith; they understood each other. The first glance exchanged by father and son expressed their affection - their veneration for that excellent woman, who in the fulness of her religious fervor, forgot, perhaps, too much the creature for the Creator.

Rose and Blanche, confused and affected, looked with interest on the kneeling woman; while Mother Bunch, shedding in silence tears of joy at the thought of Agricola's happiness, withdrew into the most obscure corner of the room, feeling that she was a stranger, and necessarily out of place in that family meeting. Frances rose, and took a step towards her husband, who received her in his arms. There was a moment of solemn silence. Dagobert and Frances said not a word. Nothing could be heard but a few sighs, mingled with sighs of joy. And, when the aged couple looked up, their expression was calm, radiant, serene; for the full and complete enjoyment of simple and pure sentiments never leaves behind a feverish and violent agitation.

"My children," said the soldier, in tones of emotion, presenting the orphans to Frances, who, after her first agitation, had surveyed them with astonishment, "this is my good and worthy wife; she will be to the daughters of General Simon what I have been to them."

"Then, madame, you will treat us as your children," said Rose, approaching Frances with her sister.

"The daughters of General Simon!" cried Dagobert's wife, more and more astonished.

"Yes, my dear Frances; I have brought them from afar not without some difficulty; but I will tell you that by and by."

"Poor little things! One would take them for two angels, exactly alike!" said Frances, contemplating the orphans with as much interest as admiration.

"Now - for us," cried Dagobert, turning to his son.

"At last," rejoined the latter.

We must renounce all attempts to describe the wild joy of Dagobert and his son, and the crushing grip of their hands, which Dagobert interrupted only to look in Agricola's face; while he rested his hands on the young blacksmith's broad shoulders that he might see to more advantage his frank masculine countenance, and robust frame. Then he shook his hand again, exclaiming, "He's a fine fellow - well built - what a good-hearted look he has!"

From a corner of the room Mother Bunch enjoyed Agricola's happiness; but she feared that her presence, till then unheeded, would be an intrusion. She wished to withdraw unnoticed, but could not do so. Dagobert and his son were between her and the door; and she stood unable to take her eyes from the charming faces of Rose and Blanche. She had never seen anything so winsome; and the extraordinary resemblance of the sisters increased her surprise. Then, their humble mourning revealing that they were poor, Mother Bunch involuntarily felt more sympathy towards them.

"Dear children! They are cold; their little hands are frozen, and, unfortunately, the fire is out," said Frances, She tried to warm the orphans' hands in hers, while Dagobert and his son gave themselves up to the feelings of affection, so long restrained.

As soon as Frances said that the fire was out, Mother Bunch hastened to make herself useful, as an excuse for her presence; and, going to the cupboard, where the charcoal and wood were kept, she took some small pieces, and, kneeling before the stove, succeeded, by the aid of a few embers that remained, in relighting the fire, which soon began to draw and blaze. Filling a coffee-pot with water, she placed it on the stove, presuming that the orphans required some warm drink. The sempstress did all this with so much dexterity and so little noise - she was naturally so forgotten amidst the emotions of the scene - that Frances, entirely occupied with Rose and Blanche, only perceived the fire when she felt its warmth diffusing round, and heard the boiling water singing in the coffee-pot. This phenomenon - fire rekindling of itself - did not astonish Dagobert's wife then, so wholly was she taken up in devising how she could lodge the maidens; for Dagobert as we have seen, had not given her notice of their arrival.

Suddenly a loud bark was heard three or four times at the door.

"Hallo! there's Spoil-sport," said Dagobert, letting in his dog; "he wants to come in to brush acquaintance with the family too."

The dog came in with a bound, and in a second was quite at home. After having rubbed Dagobert's hand with his muzzle, he went in turns to greet Rose and Blanche, and also Frances and Agricola; but seeing that they took but little notice of him, he perceived Mother Bunch, who stood apart, in an obscure corner of the room, and carrying out the popular saying, "the friends of our friends are our friends," he went and licked the hands of the young workwoman, who was just then forgotten by all. By a singular impulse, this action affected the girl to tears; she patted her long, thin, white hand several times on the head of the intelligent dog. Then, finding that she could be no longer useful (for she had done all the little services she deemed in her power), she took the handsome flower Agricola had given her, opened the door gently, and went away so discreetly that no one noticed her departure. After this exchange of mutual affection, Dagobert, his wife, and son, began to think of the realities of life.

"Poor Frances," said the soldier, glancing at Rose and Blanche, "you did not expect such a pretty surprise!"

"I am only sorry, my friend," replied Frances, "that the daughters of General Simon will not have a better lodging than this poor room; for with Agricola's garret -"

"It composes our mansion," interrupted Dagobert; "there are handsomer, it must be confessed. But be at ease; these young ladies are drilled into not being hard to suit on that score. To-morrow, I and my boy will go arm and arm, and I'll answer for it he won't walk the more upright and straight of the two, and find out General Simon's father, at M. Hardy's factory, to talk about business."

"To-morrow," said Agricola to Dagobert, "you will not find at the factory either M. Hardy or Marshall Simon's father."

"What is that you say, my lad?" cried Dagobert, hastily, "the Marshal!"

"To be sure; since 1830, General Simon's friends have secured him the title and rank which the emperor gave him at the battle of Ligny."

"Indeed!" cried Dagobert, with emotion, "but that ought not to surprise me; for, after all, it is just; and when the emperor said a thing, the least they can do is to let it abide. But it goes all the same to my heart; it makes me jump again."

Addressing the sisters, he said: "Do you hear that, my children? You arrive in Paris the daughters of a Duke and Marshal of France. One would hardly think it, indeed, to see you in this room, my poor little duchesses! But patience; all will go well. Ah, father Simon must have been very glad to hear that his son was restored to his rank! eh, my lad?"

"He told us he would renounce all kinds of ranks and titles to see his son again; for it was during the general's absence that his friends obtained this act of justice. But they expect Marshal Simon every moment, for the last letter from India announced his departure."

At these words Rose and Blanche looked at each other; and their eyes filled with tears.

"Heaven be praised! These children rely on his return; but why shall we not find M. Hardy and father Simon at the factory to-morrow?"

"Ten days ago, they went to examine and study an English mill established in the south; but we expect them back every day."

"The deuce! that's vexing; I relied on seeing the general's father, to talk over some important matters with him. At any rate, they know where to write to him. So to-morrow you will let him know, my lad, that his granddaughters are arrived. In the mean time, children," added the soldier, to Rose and Blanche, "my good wife will give you her bed and you must put up with the chances of war. Poor things! they will not be worse off here than they were on the journey."

"You know we shall always be well off with you and madame," said Rose.

"Besides, we only think of the pleasure of being at length in Paris, since here we are to find our father," added Blanche.

"That hope gives you patience, I know," said Dagobert, "but no matter! After all you have heard about it, you ought to be finely surprised, my children. As yet, you have not found it the golden city of your dreams, by any means. But, patience, patience; you'll find Paris not so bad as it looks."

"Besides," said Agricola, "I am sure the arrival of Marshal Simon in Paris will change it for you into a golden city."

"You are right, Agricola," said Rose, with a smile, "you have, indeed, guessed us."

"What! do you know my name?"

"Certainly, Agricola, we often talked about you with Dagobert; and latterly, too, with Gabriel," added Blanche.

"Gabriel!" cried Agricola and his mother, at the same time.

"Yes," replied Dagobert, making a sign of intelligence to the orphans, "we have lots to tell you for a fortnight to come; and among other things, how we chanced to meet with Gabriel. All I can now say is that, in his way, he is quite as good as my boy (I shall never be tired of saying 'my boy'); and they ought to love each other like brothers. Oh, my brave, brave wife!" said Dagobert, with emotion, "you did a good thing, poor as you were, taking the unfortunate child - and bringing him up with your own."

"Don't talk so much about it, my dear; it was such a simple thing."

"You are right; but I'll make you amends for it by and by. 'Tis down to your account; in the mean time, you will be sure to see him to-morrow morning."

"My dear brother arrived too!" cried the blacksmith; "who'll say, after this, that there are not days set apart for happiness? How came you to meet him, father?"

"I'll tell you all, by and by, about when and how we met Gabriel; for if you expect to sleep, you are mistaken. You'll give me half your room, and a fine chat we'll have. Spoil-sport will stay outside of this door; he is accustomed to sleep at the children's door."

"Dear me, love, I think of nothing. But, at such a moment, if you and the young ladies wish to sup, Agricola will fetch something from the cook-shop."

"What do you say, children?"

"No, thank you, Dagobert, we are not hungry; we are too happy."

"You will take a little wine and water, sweetened, nice and hot, to warm you a little, my dear young ladies," said Frances; "unfortunately, I have nothing else to offer you."

"You are right, Frances; the dear children are tired, and want to go to bed; while they do so, I'll go to my boy's room, and, before Rose and Blanche are awake, I will come down and converse with you, just to give Agricola a respite."

A knock was now heard at the door.

"It is good Mother Bunch come to see if we want her," said Agricola.

"But I think she was here when my husband came in," added Frances.

"Right, mother; and the good girl left lest she should be an intruder: she is so thoughtful. But no - no - it is not she who knocks so loud."

"Go and see who it is, then, Agricola."

Before the blacksmith could reach the door, a man decently dressed, with a respectable air, entered the room, and glanced rapidly round, looking for a moment at Rose and Blanche.

"Allow me to observe, sir," said Agricola, "that after knocking, you might have waited till the door was opened, before you entered. Pray, what is your business?"

"Pray excuse me, sir," said the man, very politely, and speaking slowly, perhaps to prolong his stay in the room: "I beg a thousand pardons - I regret my intrusion - I am ashamed -"

"Well, you ought to be, sir," said Agricola, with impatience, "what do you want?"

"Pray, sir, does not Miss Soliveau, a deformed needlewoman, live here?"

"No, sir; upstairs," said Agricola.

"Really, sir," cried the polite man, with low bows, "I am quite abroad at my blunder: I thought this was the room of that young person. I brought her proposals for work from a very respectable party."

"It is very late, sir," said Agricola, with surprise. "But that young person is as one of our family. Call to-morrow; you cannot see her to night; she is gone to bed."

"Then, sir, I again beg you to excuse -"

"Enough, sir," said Agricola, taking a step towards the door.

"I hope, madame and the young ladies, as well as this gent, will be assured that -"

"If you go on much longer making excuses, sir, you will have to excuse the length of your excuses; and it is time this came to an end!"

Rose and Blanche smiled at these words of Agricola; while Dagobert rubbed his moustache with pride.

"What wit the boy has!" said he aside to his wife. "But that does not astonish you - you are used to it."

During this speech, the ceremonious person withdrew, having again directed a long inquiring glance to the sisters, and to Agricola and Dagobert.

In a few minutes after, Frances having spread a mattress on the ground for herself, and put the whitest sheets on her bed for the orphans, assisted them to undress with maternal solicitude, Dagobert and Agricola having previously withdrawn to their garret. Just as the blacksmith, who preceded his father with a light, passed before the door of Mother Bunch's room, the latter, half concealed in the shade, said to him rapidly, in a low tone:

"Agricola, great danger threatens you: I must speak to you."

These words were uttered in so hasty and low a voice that Dagobert did not hear them; but as Agricola stopped suddenly, with a start, the old soldier said to him,

"Well, boy, what is it?"

"Nothing, father," said the blacksmith, turning round; "I feared I did not light you well."

"Oh, stand at ease about that; I have the legs and eyes of fifteen to night;" and the soldier, not noticing his son's surprise, went into the little room where they were both to pass the night.

On leaving the house, after his inquiries about Mother Bunch, the over polite Paul Pry slunk along to the end of Brise-Miche Street. He advanced towards a hackney-coach drawn up on the Cloitre Saint-Merry Square.

In this carriage lounged Rodin, wrapped in a cloak.

"Well?" said he, in an inquiring tone.

"The two girls and the man with gray moustache went directly to Frances Baudoin's; by listening at the door, I learnt that the sisters will sleep with her, in that room, to-night; the old man with gray moustache will share the young blacksmith's room."

"Very well," said Rodin.

"I did not dare insist on seeing the deformed workwoman this evening on the subject of the Bacchanal Queen; I intend returning to-morrow, to learn the effect of the letter she must have received this evening by the post about the young blacksmith."

"Do not fail! And now you will call, for me, on Frances Baudoin's confessor, late as it is; you will tell him that I am waiting for him at Rue du Milieu des Ursins - he must not lose a moment. Do you come with him. Should I not be returned, he will wait for me. You will tell him it is on a matter of great moment."

"All shall be faithfully executed," said the ceremonious man, cringing to Rodin, as the coach drove quickly away.

CHAPTER XXXI

AGRICOLA AND MOTHER BUNCH

Within one hour after the different scenes which have just been described the most profound silence reigned in the soldier's humble dwelling. A flickering light, which played through two panes of glass in a door, betrayed that Mother Bunch had not yet gone to sleep; for her gloomy recess, without air or light, was impenetrable to the rays of day, except by this door, opening upon a narrow and obscure passage, connected with the roof. A sorry bed, a table, an old portmanteau, and a chair, so nearly filled this chilling abode, that two persons could not possibly be seated within it, unless one of them sat upon the side of the bed.

The magnificent and precious flower that Agricola had given to the girl was carefully stood up in a vessel of water, placed upon the table on a linen cloth, diffusing its sweet odor around, and expanding its purple calix in the very closet, whose plastered walls, gray and damp, were feebly lighted by the rays of an attenuated candle. The sempstress, who had taken off no part of her dress, was seated upon her bed - her looks were downcast, and her eyes full of tears. She supported herself with one hand resting on the bolster; and, inclining towards the door, listened with painful eagerness, every instant hoping to hear the footsteps of Agricola. The heart of the young sempstress beat violently; her face, usually very pale, was now partially flushed - so exciting was the emotion by which she was agitated. Sometimes she cast her eyes with terror upon a letter which she held in her hand, a letter that had been delivered by post in the course of the evening, and which had been placed by the housekeeper (the dyer) upon the table, while she was rendering some trivial domestic services during the recognitions of Dagobert and his family.

After some seconds, Mother Bunch heard a door, very near her own, softly opened.

"There he is at last!" she exclaimed, and Agricola immediately entered.

"I waited till my father went to sleep," said the blacksmith, in a low voice, his physiognomy evincing much more curiosity than uneasiness. "But what is the matter, my good sister? How your countenance is changed! You weep! What has happened? About what danger would you speak to me?"

"Hush! Read this!" said she, her voice trembling with emotion, while she hastily presented to him the open letter. Agricola held it towards the light, and read what follows:

"A person who has reasons for concealing himself, but who knows the sisterly interest you take in the welfare of Agricola Baudoin, warns you. That young and worthy workman will probably be arrested in the course of to-morrow."

"I!" exclaimed Agricola, looking at Mother Bunch with an air of stupefied amazement. "What is the meaning of all this?"

"Read on!" quickly replied the sempstress, clasping her hands.

Agricola resumed reading, scarcely believing the evidence of his eyes:-"The song, entitled 'Working-men Freed,' has been declared libellous. Numerous copies of it have been found among the papers of a secret society, the leaders of which are about to be incarcerated, as being concerned in the Rue des Prouvaires conspiracy."

"Alas!" said the girl, melting into tears, "now I see it all. The man who was lurking about below, this evening, who was observed by the dyer, was, doubtless, a spy, lying in wait for you coming home."

"Nonsense!" exclaimed Agricola. "This accusation is quite ridiculous! Do not torment yourself. I never trouble myself with politics. My verses breathe nothing but philanthropy. Am I to blame, if they have been found among the papers of a secret society?" Agricola disdainfully threw the letter upon the table.

"Read! pray read!" said the other; "read on."

"If you wish it," said Agricola, "I will; no time is lost."

He resumed the reading of the letter:

"A warrant is about to be issued against Agricola Baudoin. There is mo doubt of his innocence being sooner or later made clear; but it will be well if he screen himself for a time as much as possible from pursuit, in order that he may escape a confinement of two or three months previous to trial - an imprisonment which would be a terrible blow for his mother, whose sole support he is.

"A SINCERE FRIEND, who is compelled to remain unknown."

After a moment's silence, the blacksmith raised his head; his countenance resumed its serenity; and laughing, he said: "Reassure yourself, good Mother Bunch, these jokers have made a mistake by trying their games on me. It is plainly an attempt at making an April-fool of me before the time."

"Agricola, for the love of heaven!" said the girl, in a supplicating tone; "treat not the warning thus lightly. Believe in my forebodings, and listen to my advice."

"I tell you again, my good girl," replied Agricola, "that it is two months since my song was published. It is not in any way political; indeed, if it were, they would not have waited till now before coming down on me."

"But," said the other, "you forget that new events have arisen. It is scarcely two days since the conspiracy was discovered, in this very neighborhood, in the Rue des Prouvaires. And," continued she, "if the verses, though perhaps hitherto unnoticed, have now been found in the possession of the persons apprehended for this conspiracy, nothing more is necessary to compromise you in the plot."

"Compromise me!" said Agricola; "my verses! in which I only praise the love of labor and of goodness! To arrest me for that! If so, justice would be but a blind noodle. That she might grope her way, it would be necessary to furnish her with a dog and a pilgrim's staff to guide her steps."

"Agricola," resumed Mother Bunch; overwhelmed with anxiety and terror on hearing the blacksmith jest at such a moment, "I conjure you to listen to me! No doubt you uphold in the verses the sacred love of labor; but you do also grievously deplore and deprecate the unjust lot of the poor laborers, devoted as they are, without hope, to all the miseries of life; you recommend, indeed, only fraternity among men; but your good and noble heart vents its indignation, at the same time, against the selfish and the wicked. In fine, you fervently hasten on, with the ardor of your wishes, the emancipation of all the artisans who, less fortunate than you, have not generous M. Hardy for employer. Say, Agricola, in these times of trouble, is there anything more necessary to compromise you than that numerous copies of your song have been found in possession of the persons who have been apprehended?"

Agricola was moved by these affectionate and judicious expressions of an excellent creature, who reasoned from her heart; and he began to view with more seriousness the advice which she had given him.

Perceiving that she had shaken him, the sewing-girl went on to say: "And then, bear your fellow-workman, Remi, in recollection."

"Remi!" said Agricola, anxiously.

"Yes," resumed the sempstress; "a letter of his, a letter in itself quite insignificant, was found in the house of a person arrested last year for conspiracy; and Remi, in consequence, remained a month in prison."

"That is true, but the injustice of his implication was easily shown, and he was set at liberty."

"Yes, Agricola: but not till he had lain a month in prison; and that has furnished the motive of the person who advised you to conceal yourself! A month in prison! Good heavens! Agricola, think of that! and your mother."

These words made a powerful impression upon Agricola. He took up the letter and again read it attentively.

"And the man who has been lurking all this evening about the house?" proceeded she. "I constantly recall that circumstance, which cannot be naturally accounted for. Alas! what a blow it would be for your father, and poor mother, who is incapable of earning anything. Are you not now their only resource? Oh! consider, then, what would become of them without you - without your labor!"

"It would indeed be terrible," said Agricola, impatiently casting the letter upon the table. "What you have said concerning Remi is too true. He was as innocent as I am: yet an error of justice, an involuntary error though it be, is not the less cruel. But they don't commit a man without hearing him."

"But they arrest him first, and hear him afterwards," said Mother Bunch, bitterly; "and then, after a month or two, they restore him his liberty. And if he have a wife and children, whose only means of living is his daily labor, what becomes of them while their only supporter is in prison? They suffer hunger, they endure cold, and they weep!"

At these simple and pathetic words, Agricola trembled.

"A month without work," he said, with a sad and thoughtful air. "And my mother, and father, and the two young ladies who make part of our family until the arrival in Paris of their father, Marshal Simon. Oh! you are right. That thought, in spite of myself, affrights me!"

"Agricola!" exclaimed the girl impetuously; "suppose you apply to M. Hardy; he is so good, and his character is so much esteemed and honored, that, if he offered bail for you, perhaps they would give up their persecution?"

"Unfortunately," replied Agricola, "M. Hardy is absent; he is on a journey with Marshal Simon."

After a silence of some time, Agricola, striving to surmount his fear, added: "But no! I cannot give credence to this letter. After all, I had rather await what may come. I'll at least have the chance of proving my innocence on my first examination: for indeed, my good sister, whether it be that I am in prison or that I fly to conceal myself, my working for my family will be equally prevented."

"Alas! that is true," said the poor girl; "what is to be done! Oh, what is to be done?"

"My brave father," said Agricola to himself, "if this misfortune happen to-morrow, what an awakening it will be for him, who came here to sleep so joyously!" The blacksmith buried his face in his hands.

Unhappily Mother Bunch's fears were too well-founded, for it will be recollected that at that epoch of the year 1832, before and after the Rue des Prouvaires conspiracy, a very great number of arrests had been made among the working classes, in consequence of a violent reaction against democratical ideas.

Suddenly, the girl broke the silence which had been maintained for some seconds. A blush colored her features, which bore the impressions of an indefinable expression of constraint, grief, and hope.

"Agricola, you are saved!"

"What say you?" he asked.

"The young lady, so beautiful, so good, who gave you this flower" (she showed it to the blacksmith) "who has known how to make reparation with so much delicacy for having made a painful offer, cannot but have a generous heart. You must apply to her -"

With these words which seemed to be wrung from her by a violent effort over herself, great tears rolled down her cheeks. For the first time in her life she experienced a feeling of grievous jealousy. Another woman was so happy as to have the power of coming to the relief of him whom she idolized; while she herself, poor creature, was powerless and wretched.

"Do you think so?" exclaimed Agricola surprised. "But what could be done with this young lady?"

"Did she not say to you," answered Mother Bunch, "'Remember my name; and in all circumstances address yourself to me?'"

"She did indeed!" replied Agricola.

"This young lady, in her exalted position, ought to have powerful connections who will be able to protect and defend you. Go to her to morrow morning; tell her frankly what has happened, and request her support."

"But tell me, my good sister, what it is you wish me to do?"

"Listen. I remember that, in former times, my father told us that he had saved one of his friends from being put in prison, by becoming surety for him. It will be easy for you so to convince this young lady of your innocence, that she will be induced to become surety; and after that, you will have nothing more to fear."

"My poor child!" said Agricola, "to ask so great a service from a person to whom one is almost unknown is hard."

"Believe me, Agricola," said the other sadly, "I would never counsel what could possibly lower you in the eyes of any one, and above all - do you understand? - above all, in the eyes of this young lady. I do not propose that you should ask money from her; but only that she should give surety for you, in order that you may have the liberty of continuing at your employment, so that the family may not be without resources. Believe me, Agricola, that such a request is in no respect inconsistent with what is noble and becoming upon your part. The heart of the young lady is generous. She will comprehend your position. The required surety will be as nothing to her; while to you it will be everything, and will even be the very life to those who depend upon you."

"You are right, my good sister," said Agricola, with sadness and dejection. "It is perhaps worth while to risk taking this step. If the young lady consent to render me this service, and if giving surety will indeed preserve me from prison, I shall be prepared for every event. But no, no!" added he, rising, "I'd never dare to make the request to her! What right have I to do so? What is the insignificant service that I rendered her, when compared with that which I should solicit from her?"

"Do you imagine then, Agricola, that a generous spirit measures the services which ought to be rendered, by those previously received? Trust to me respecting a matter which is an affair of the heart. I am, it is true, but a lowly creature, and ought not to compare myself with any other person. I am nothing, and I can do nothing. Nevertheless, I am sure - yes, Agricola, I am sure - that this young lady, who is so very far above me, will experience the same feelings that I do in this affair; yes, like me, she will at once comprehend that your position is a cruel one; and she will do with joy, with happiness, with thankfulness, that which I would do, if, alas! I could do anything more than uselessly consume myself with regrets."

In spite of herself, she pronounced the last words with an expression so heart-breaking - there was something so moving in the comparison which this unfortunate creature, obscure and disdained, infirm and miserable, made of herself with Adrienne de Cardoville, the very type of resplendent youth, beauty, and opulence - that Agricola was moved even to tears; and, holding out one of his hands to the speaker, he said to her, tenderly, "How very good you are; how full of nobleness, good feeling, and delicacy!"

"Unhappily," said the weeping girl, "I can do nothing more than advise."

"And your counsels shall be followed out, my sister dear. They are those of a soul the most elevated I have ever known. Yes, you have won me over into making this experiment, by persuading me that the heart of Miss de Cardoville is perhaps equal in value to your own!"

At this charming and sincere assimilation of herself to Miss Adrienne, the sempstress forgot almost everything she had suffered, so exquisitely sweet and consoling were her emotions. If some poor creatures, fatally devoted to sufferings, experience griefs of which the world knows naught, they sometimes, too, are cheered by humble and timid joys, of which the world is equally ignorant. The least word of true tenderness and affection, which elevates them in their own estimation, is ineffably blissful for these unfortunate beings, habitually consigned, not only to hardships and to disdain, but even to desolating doubts, and distrust of themselves.

"Then it is agreed that you will go, to-morrow morning to this young lady's house?" exclaimed Mother Bunch, trembling with a new-born hope. "And," she quickly added, "at break of day I'll go down to watch at the street-door, to see if there be anything suspicious, and to apprise you of what I perceive."

"Good, excellent girl!" exclaimed Agricola, with increasing emotion.

"It will be necessary to endeavor to set off before the wakening of your father," said the hunchback. "The quarter in which the young lady dwells, is so deserted, that the mere going there will almost serve for your present concealment."

"I think I hear the voice of my father," said Agricola suddenly.

In truth, the little apartment was so near Agricola's garret, that he and the sempstress, listening, heard Dagobert say in the dark:

"Agricola, is it thus that you sleep, my boy? Why, my first sleep is over; and my tongue itches deucedly."

"Go quick, Agricola!" said Mother Bunch; "your absence would disquiet him. On no account go out to-morrow morning, before I inform you whether or not I shall have seen anything suspicious."

"Why, Agricola, you are not here?" resumed Dagobert, in a louder voice.

"Here I am, father," said the smith, while going out of the sempstress's apartment, and entering the garret, to his father.

"I have been to fasten the shutter of a loft that the wind agitated, lest its noise should disturb you."

"Thanks, my boy; but it is not noise that wakes me," said Dagobert, gayly; "it is an appetite, quite furious, for a chat with you. Oh, my dear boy, it is the hungering of a proud old man of a father, who has not seen his son for eighteen years."

"Shall I light a candle, father?"

"No, no; that would be luxurious; let us chat in the dark. It will be a new pleasure for me to see you to-morrow morning at daybreak. It will be like seeing you for the first time twice." The door of Agricola's garret being now closed, Mother Bunch heard nothing more.

The poor girl, without undressing, threw herself upon the bed, and closed not an eye during the night, painfully awaiting the appearance of day, in order that she might watch over the safety of Agricola. However, in spite of her vivid anxieties for the morrow, she sometimes allowed herself to sink into the reveries of a bitter melancholy. She compared the conversation she had just had in the silence of night, with the man whom she secretly adored, with what that conversation might have been, had she possessed some share of charms and beauty - had she been loved as she loved, with a chaste and devoted flame! But soon sinking into belief that she should never know the ravishing sweets of a mutual passion, she found consolation in the hope of being useful to Agricola. At the dawn of day, she rose softly, and descended the staircase with little noise, in order to see if anything menaced Agricola from without.

CHAPTER XXXII

THE AWAKENING

The weather, damp and foggy during a portion of the night, became clear and cold towards morning. Through the glazed skylight of Agricola's garret, where he lay with his father, a corner of the blue sky could be seen.

The apartment of the young blacksmith had an aspect as poor as the sewing-girl's. For its sole ornament, over the deal table upon which Agricola wrote his poetical inspirations, there hung suspended from a nail in the wall a portrait of Beranger - that immortal poet whom the people revere and cherish, because his rare and transcendent genius has delighted to enlighten the people, and to sing their glories and their reverses.

Although the day had only begun to dawn, Dagobert and Agricola had already risen. The latter had sufficient self command to conceal his inquietude, for renewed reflection had again increased his fears.

The recent outbreak in the Rue des Prouvaires had caused a great number of precautionary arrests; and the discovery of numerous copies of Agricola's song, in the possession of one of the chiefs of the disconcerted plot, was, in truth, calculated slightly to compromise the young blacksmith. His father, however, as we have already mentioned, suspected not his secret anguish. Seated by the side of his son, upon the edge of their mean little bed, the old soldier, by break of day, had dressed and shaved with military care; he now held between his hands both those of Agricola, his countenance radiant with joy, and unable to discontinue the contemplation of his boy.

"You will laugh at me, my dear boy," said Dagobert to his son; "but I wished the night to the devil, in order that I might gaze upon you in full day, as I now see you. But all in good time; I have lost nothing. Here is another silliness of mine; it delights me to see you wear moustaches. What a splendid horse-grenadier you would have made! Tell me; have you never had a wish to be a soldier?"

"I thought of mother!"

"That's right," said Dagobert: "and besides, I believe, after all, look ye, that the time of the sword has gone by. We old fellows are now good for nothing, but to be put in a corner of the chimney. Like rusty old carbines, we have had our day."

"Yes; your days of heroism and of glory," said Agricola with excitement; and then he added, with a voice profoundly softened and agitated, "it is something good and cheering to be your son!"

"As to the good, I know nothing of that," replied Dagobert; "but as for the cheering, it ought to be so; for I love you proudly. And I think this is but the beginning! What say you, Agricola? I am like the famished wretches who have been some days without food. It is but by little and little that they recover themselves, and can eat. Now, you may expect to be tasted, my boy, morning and evening, and devoured during the day. No, I wish not to think that - not all the day - no, that thought dazzles and perplexes me; and I am no longer myself."

These words of Dagobert caused a painful feeling to Agricola. He believed that they sprang from a presentiment of the separation with which he was menaced.

"Well," continued Dagobert; "you are quite happy; M. Hardy is always good to you."

"Oh!" replied Agricola: "there is none in the world better, or more equitable and generous! If you knew what wonders he has brought about in his factory! Compared to all others, it is a paradise beside the stithies of Lucifer!"

"Indeed!" said Dagobert.

"You shall see," resumed Agricola, "what welfare, what joy, what affection, are displayed upon the countenances of all whom he employs; who work with an ardent pleasure.

"This M. Hardy of yours must be an out-and-out magician," said Dagobert.

"He is, father, a very great magician. He has known how to render labor pleasant and attractive. As for the pleasure, over and above good wages, he accords to us a portion of his profits according to our deserts; whence you may judge of the eagerness with which we go to work. And that is not all: he has caused large, handsome buildings to be erected, in which all his workpeople find, at less expense than elsewhere, cheerful and salubrious lodgings, in which they enjoy all the advantages of an association. But you shall see - I repeat - you shall see!"

"They have good reason to say, that Paris is the region of wonders," observed Dagobert.

"Well, behold me here again at last, never more to quit you, nor good mother!"

"No, father, we will never separate again," said Agricola, stifling a sigh. "My mother and I will both try to make you forget all that you have suffered."

"Suffered!" exclaimed Dagobert, "who the deuce has suffered? Look me well in the face; and see if I have a look of suffering!

Bombs and bayonets! Since I have put my foot here, I feel myself quite a young man again! You shall see me march soon: I bet that I tire you out! You must rig yourself up something extra! Lord, how they will stare at us! I wager that in beholding your black moustache and my gray one, folks will say, behold father and son! But let us settle what we are to do with the day. You will write to the father of Marshal Simon, informing him the his grand-daughters have arrived, and that it is necessary that he should hasten his return to Paris; for he has charged himself with matters which are of great importance for them. While you are writing, I will go down to say good-morning to my wife, and to the dear little ones. We will then eat a morsel. Your mother will go to mass; for I perceive that she likes to be regular at that: the good soul! no great harm, if it amuse her! and during her absence, we will make a raid together."

"Father," said Agricola, with embarrassment, "this morning it is out of my power to accompany you."

"How! out of your power?" said Dagobert; "recollect this is Monday!"

"Yes, father," said Agricola, hesitatingly; "but I have promised to attend all the morning in the workshop, to finish a job that is required in a hurry. If I fail to do so, I shall inflict some injury upon M. Hardy. But I'll soon be at liberty."

"That alters the case," said Dagobert, with a sigh of regret. "I thought to make my first parade through Paris with you this morning; but it must be deferred in favor of your work. It is sacred: since it is that which sustains your mother. Nevertheless, it is vexatious, devilish vexatious. And yet no - I am unjust. See how quickly one gets habituated to and spoilt by happiness. I growl like a true grumbler, at a walk being put off for a few hours! I do this! I who, during eighteen years, have only hoped to see you once more, without daring to reckon very much upon it! Oh! I am but a silly old fool! Vive l'amour et cogni - I mean - my Agricola!" And, to console himself, the old soldier gayly slapped his son's shoulder.

This seemed another omen of evil to the blacksmith; for he dreaded one moment to another lest the fears of Mother Bunch should be realized. "Now that I have recovered myself," said Dagobert, laughing, "let us speak of business. Know you where I find the addresses of all the notaries in Paris?"

"I don't know; but nothing is more easy than to discover it."

"My reason is," resumed Dagobert, "that I sent from Russia by post, and by order of the mother of the two children that I have brought here, some important papers to a Parisian notary. As it was my duty to see this notary immediately upon my arrival, I had written his name and his address in a portfolio, of which however, I have been robbed during my journey; and as I have forgotten his devil of a name, it seems to me, that if I should see it again in the list of notaries, I might recollect it."

Two knocks at the door of the garret made Agricola start. He involuntarily thought of a warrant for his apprehension.

His father, who, at the sound of the knocking turned round his head, had not perceived his emotion, and said with a loud voice: "Come in!" The door opened. It was Gabriel. He wore a black cassock and a broad brimmed hat.

To recognize his brother by adoption, and to throw himself into his arms, were two movements performed at once by Agricola - as quick as thought. - "My brother!" exclaimed Agricola.

"Agricola!" cried Gabriel.

"Gabriel!" responded the blacksmith.

"After so long an absence!" said the one.

"To behold you again!" rejoined the other.

Such were the words exchanged between the blacksmith and

the missionary, while they were locked in a close embrace.

Dagobert, moved and charmed by these fraternal endearments, felt his eyes become moist. There was something truly touching in the affection of the young men - in their hearts so much alike, and yet of characters and aspects so very different - for the manly countenance of Agricola contrasted strongly with the delicacy and angelic physiognomy of Gabriel.

"I was forewarned by my father of your arrival," said the blacksmith at length. "I have been expecting to see you; and my happiness has been a hundred times the greater, because I have had all the pleasures of hoping for it."

"And my good mother?" asked Gabriel, in affectionately grasping the hands of Dagobert. "I trust that you have found her in good health."

"Yes, my brave boy!" replied Dagobert; "and her health will have become a hundred times better, now that we are all together. Nothing is so healthful as joy." Then addressing himself to Agricola, who, forgetting his fear of being arrested, regarded the missionary with an expression of ineffable affection, Dagobert added:

"Let it be remembered, that, with the soft cheek of a young girl, Gabriel has the courage of a lion; I have already told with what intrepidity he saved the lives of Marshal Simon's daughters, and tried to save mine also."

"But, Gabriel! what has happened to your forehead?" suddenly exclaimed Agricola, who for a few seconds had been attentively examining the missionary.

Gabriel, having thrown aside his hat on entering, was now directly beneath the skylight of the garret apartment, the bright light through which shone upon his sweet, pale countenance: and the round scar, which extended from one eyebrow to the other, was therefore distinctly visible.

In the midst of the powerful and diversified emotion, and of the exciting events which so rapidly followed the shipwreck on the rocky coast near Cardoville House, Dagobert, during the short interview he then had with Gabriel, had not perceived the scar which seamed the forehead of the young missionary. Now, partaking, however, of the surprise of his son, Dagobert said:

"Aye, indeed! how came this scar upon your brow?"

"And on his hands, too; see, dear father!" exclaimed the blacksmith, with renewed surprise, while he seized one of the hands which the young priest held out towards him in order to tranquillize his fears.

"Gabriel, my brave boy, explain this to us!" added Dagobert; "who has wounded you thus?" and in his turn, taking the other hand of the missionary, he examined the scar upon it with the eye of a judge of wounds, and then added, "In Spain, one of my comrades was found and taken down alive from a cross, erected at the junction of several roads, upon which the monks had crucified, and left him to die of hunger, thirst, and agony. Ever afterwards he bore scars upon his hands, exactly similar to this upon your hand."

"My father is right!" exclaimed Agricola. "It is evident that your hands have been pierced through! My poor brother!" and Agricola became grievously agitated.

"Do not think about it," said Gabriel, reddening with the embarrassment of modesty. "Having gone as a missionary amongst the savages of the Rocky Mountains, they crucified me, and they had begun to scalp me, when Providence snatched me from their hands."

"Unfortunate youth," said Dagobert; "without arms then? You had not a sufficient escort for your protection?"

"It is not for such as me to carry arms." said Gabriel, sweetly smiling; "and we are never accompanied by any escort."

"Well, but your companions, those who were along with you, how came it that they did not defend you?" impetuously asked Agricola.

"I was alone, my dear brother."

"Alone!"

"Yes, alone; without even a guide."

"You alone! unarmed! in a barbarous country!" exclaimed Dagobert, scarcely crediting a step so unmilitary, and almost distrusting his own sense of hearing.

"It was sublime!" said the young blacksmith and poet.

"The Christian faith," said Gabriel, with mild simplicity, "cannot be implanted by force or violence. It is only by the power of persuasion that the gospel can be spread amongst poor savages."

"But when persuasions fail!" said Agricola.

"Why, then, dear brother, one has but to die for the belief that is in him, pitying those who have rejected it, and who have refused the blessings it offers to mankind."

There was a period of profound silence after the reply of Gabriel, which was uttered with simple and touching pathos.

Dagobert was in his own nature too courageous not to comprehend a heroism thus calm and resigned; and the old soldier, as well as his son, now contemplated Gabriel with the most earnest feelings of mingled admiration and respect.

Gabriel, entirely free from the affection of false modesty, seemed quite unconscious of the emotions which he had excited in the breasts of his two friends; and he therefore said to Dagobert, "What ails you?"

"What ails me!" exclaimed the brave old soldier, with great emotion: "After having been for thirty years in the wars, I had imagined myself to be about as courageous as any man. And now I find I have a master! And that master is yourself!"

"I!" said Gabriel; "what do you mean? What have I done?"

"Thunder, don't you know that the brave wounds there" (the veteran took with transport both of Gabriel's hands), "that these wounds are as glorious - are more glorious than our - than all ours, as warriors by profession!"

"Yes! yes, my father speaks truth!" exclaimed Agricola; and he added, with enthusiasm, "Oh, for such priests! How I love them! How I venerate them! How I am elevated by their charity, their courage, their resignation!"

"I entreat you not to extol me thus," said Gabriel with embarrassment.

"Not extol you!" replied Dagobert. "Hanged if I shouldn't. When I have gone into the heat of action, did I rush into it alone? Was I not under the eyes of my commanding officer? Were not my comrades there along with me? In default of true courage, had I not the instinct of self preservation to spur me on, without reckoning the excitement of the shouts and tumult of battle, the smell of the gunpowder, the flourishes of the trumpets, the thundering of the cannon, the ardor of my horse, which bounded beneath me as if the devil were at his tail? Need I state that I also knew that the emperor was present, with his eye upon every one - the emperor, who, in recompense for a hole being made in my tough hide, would give me a bit of lace or a ribbon, as plaster for the wound. Thanks to all these causes, I passed for game. Fair enough! But are you not a thousand times more game than I, my brave boy; going alone, unarmed, to confront enemies a hundred times more ferocious than those whom we attacked - we, who fought in whole squadrons, supported by artillery, bomb-shells, and case-shot?"

"Excellent father!" cried Agricola, "how noble of you to render to Gabriel this justice!"

"Oh, dear brother," said Gabriel, "his kindness to me makes him magnify what was quite natural and simple!"

"Natural!" said the veteran soldier; "yes, natural for gallants who have hearts of the true temper: but that temper is rare."

"Oh, yes, very rare," said Agricola; "for that kind of courage is the most admirable of all. Most bravely did you seek almost certain death, alone, bearing the cross in hand as your only weapon, to preach charity and Christian brotherhood. They seized you, tortured you; and you await death and partly endure it, without complaint, without remonstrance, without hatred, without anger, without a wish for vengeance; forgiveness issuing from your mouth, and a smile of pity beaming upon your lips; and this in the depths of forests, where no one could witness your magnanimity, - none could behold you - and without other desire, after you were rescued than modestly to conceal blessed wounds under your black robe! My father is right, by Jove! can you still contend that you are not as brave as he?"

"And besides, too," resumed Dagobert, "the dear boy did all that for a thankless paymaster; for it is true, Agricola, that his wounds will never change his humble black robe of a priest into the rich robe of a bishop!"

"I am not so disinterested as I may seem to be," said Gabriel to Dagobert, smiling meekly. "If I am deemed worthy, a great recompense awaits me on high."

"As to all that, my boy," said Dagobert, "I do not understand it; and I will not argue about it. I maintain it, that my old cross of honor would be at least as deservedly affixed to your cassock as upon my uniform."

"But these recompenses are never conferred upon humble priests like Gabriel," said Agricola, "and if you did know, dear father, how much virtue and valor is among those whom the highest orders in the priesthood insolently call the inferior clergy, - the unseen merit and the blind devotedness to be found amongst worthy, but obscure, country curates, who are inhumanly treated and subjugated to a pitiless yoke by the lordly lawnsleeves! Like us, those poor priests are worthy laborers in their vocation; and for them, also, all generous hearts ought to demand enfranchisement! Sons of common people, like ourselves, and useful as we are, justice ought to be rendered both to them and to us. Do I say right, Gabriel? You will not contradict it; for you have told me, that your ambition would have been to obtain a small country curacy; because you understand the good that you could work within it."

"My desire is still the same," said Gabriel sadly: "but unfortunately -" and then, as if he wished to escape from a painful thought, and to change the conversation, he, addressing himself to Dagobert, added: "Believe me: be more just than to undervalue your own courage by exalting mine. Your courage must be very great - very great; for, after a battle, the spectacle of the carnage must be truly terrible to a generous and feeling heart. We, at least, though we may be killed, do not kill."

At these words of the missionary, the soldier drew himself up erect, looked upon Gabriel with astonishment, and said, "This is most surprising!"

"What is?" inquired Agricola.

"What Gabriel has just told us," replied Dagobert, "brings to my mind what I experienced in warfare on the battlefield in proportion as I advanced in years. Listen, my children: more than once, on the night after a general engagement, I have been mounted as a vidette, - alone, - by night, - amid the moonlight, on the field of battle which remained in our possession, and upon which lay the bodies of seven or eight thousand of the slain, amongst whom were mingled the slaughtered remains of some of my old comrades: and then this sad scene, when the profound silence has restored me to my senses from the thirst for bloodshed and the delirious whirling of my sword (intoxicated like the rest), I have said to myself, 'for what have these men been killed? - FOR WHAT - FOR WHAT?' But this feeling, well understood as it was, hindered me not, on the following morning, when the trumpets again sounded the charge, from rushing once more to the slaughter. But the same thought always recurred when my arm became weary with carnage; and after wiping my sabre upon the mane of my horse, I have said to myself, 'I have killed! - killed!! - killed!!! and, FOR WHAT!!!'"

The missionary and the blacksmith exchanged looks on hearing the old soldier give utterance to this singular retrospection of the past.

"Alas!" said Gabriel to him, "all generous hearts feel as you did during the solemn moments, when the intoxication of glory has subsided, and man is left alone to the influence of the good instincts planted in his bosom."

"And that should prove, my brave boy," rejoined Dagobert, "that you are greatly better than I; for those noble instincts, as you call them, have never abandoned you. * * * * But how the deuce did you escape from the claws of the infuriated savages who had already crucified you?"

At this question of Dagobert, Gabriel started and reddened so visibly, that the soldier said to him: "If you ought not or cannot answer my request, let us say no more about it."

"I have nothing to conceal, either from you or from my brother," replied the missionary with altered voice. "Only; it will be difficult for me to make you comprehend what I cannot comprehend myself."

"How is that?" asked Agricola with surprise.

"Surely," said Gabriel, reddening more deeply, "I must have been deceived by a fallacy of my senses, during that abstracted moment in which I awaited death with resignation. My enfeebled mind, in spite of me, must have been cheated by an illusion; or that, which to the present hour has remained inexplicable, would have been more slowly developed; and I should have known with greater certainty that it was the strange woman -"

Dagobert, while listening to the missionary, was perfectly amazed; for he also had vainly tried to account for the unexpected succor which had freed him and the two orphans from the prison at Leipsic.

"Of what woman do you speak?" asked Agricola.

"Of her who saved me," was the reply.

"A woman saved you from the hands of the savages?" said Dagobert.

"Yes," replied Gabriel, though absorbed in his reflections, "a woman, young and beautiful!"

"And who was this woman?" asked Agricola.

"I know not. When I asked her, she replied, 'I am the sister of the distressed!'"

"And whence came she? Whither went she?" asked Dagobert, singularly interested.

"'I go wheresoever there is suffering,' she replied," answered the missionary; "and she departed, going towards the north of America - towards those desolate regions in which there is eternal snow, where the nights are without end."

"As in Siberia," said Dagobert, who had become very thoughtful.

"But," resumed Agricola, addressing himself to Gabriel, who seemed also to have become more and more absorbed, "in what manner or by what means did this woman come to your assistance?"

The missionary was about to reply to the last question, when there was heard a gentle tap at the door of the garret apartment, which renewed the fears that Agricola had forgotten since the arrival of his adopted brother. "Agricola," said a sweet voice outside the door, "I wish to speak with you as soon as possible."

The blacksmith recognized Mother Bunch's voice, and opened the door. But the young sempstress, instead of entering, drew back into the dark passage, and said, with a voice of anxiety: "Agricola, it is an hour since broad day, and you have not yet departed! How imprudent! I have been watching below, in the street, until now, and have seen nothing alarming; but they may come any instant to arrest you. Hasten, I conjure you, your departure for the abode of Miss de Cardoville. Not a minute should be lost."

"Had it not been for the arrival of Gabriel, I should have been gone. But I could not resist the happiness of remaining some little time with him."

"Gabriel here!" said Mother Bunch, with sweet surprise; for, as has been stated, she had been brought up with him and Agricola.

"Yes," answered Agricola, "for half an hour he has been with my father and me."

"What happiness I shall have in seeing him again," said the sewing-girl. "He doubtless came upstairs while I had gone for a brief space to your mother, to ask if I could be useful in any way on account of the young ladies; but they have been so fatigued that they still sleep. Your mother has requested me to give you this letter for your father. She has just received it."

"Thanks."

"Well," resumed Mother Bunch, "now that you have seen Gabriel, do not delay long. Think what a blow it would be for your father, if they came to arrest you in his very presence mon Dieu!"

"You are right," said Agricola; "it is indispensable that I should depart - while near Gabriel in spite of my anxiety, my fears were forgotten."

"Go quickly, then; and if Miss de Cardoville should grant this favor, perhaps in a couple of hours you will return, quite at ease both as to yourself and us."

"True! a very few minutes more; and I'll come down."

"I return to watch at the door. If I perceive anything. I'll come up again to apprise you. But pray, do not delay."

"Be easy, good sister." Mother Bunch hurriedly descended the staircase, to resume her watch at the street door, and Agricola re-entered his garret. "Dear father," he said to Dagobert, "my mother has just received this letter, and she requests you to read it."

"Very well; read it for me, my boy." And Agricola read as follows:

"MADAME. - I understand that your husband has been charged by General Simon with an affair of very great importance. Will you, as soon as your husband arrives in Paris, request him to come to my office at Chartres without a moment's delay. I am instructed to deliver to himself, and to no other person, some documents indispensable to the interests of General Simon.

"DURAND, Notary at Chartres."

Dagobert looked at his son with astonishment, and said to him, "Who can have told this gentleman already of my arrival in Paris?"

"Perhaps, father," said Agricola, "this is the notary to whom you transmitted some papers, and whose address you have lost."

"But his name was not Durand; and I distinctly recollect that his address was Paris, not Chartres. And, besides," said the soldier, thoughtfully, "if he has some important documents, why didn't he transmit them to me?"

"It seems to me that you ought not to neglect going to him as soon as possible," said Agricola, secretly rejoiced that this circumstance would withdraw his father for about two days, during which time his (Agricola's) fate would be decided in one way or other.

"Your counsel is good," replied his father.

"This thwarts your intentions in some degree?" asked Gabriel.

"Rather, my lads; for I counted upon passing the day with you. However, 'duty before everything.' Having come happily from Siberia to Paris, it is not for me to fear a journey from Paris to Chartres, when it is required on an affair of importance. In twice twenty-four hours I shall be back again. But the deuce take me if I expected to leave Paris for Chartres to-day. Luckily, I leave Rose and Blanche with my good wife; and Gabriel, their angel, as they call him, will be here to keep them company."

"That is, unfortunately, impossible," said the missionary, sadly. "This visit on my arrival is also a farewell visit."

"A farewell visit! Now!" exclaimed Dagobert and Agricola both at once.

"Alas, yes!"

"You start already on another mission?" said Dagobert; "surely it is not possible?"

"I must answer no question upon this subject," said Gabriel, suppressing a sigh: "but from now, for some time, I cannot, and ought not, come again into this house."

"Why, my brave boy," resumed Dagobert with emotion, "there is something in thy conduct that savors of constraint, of oppression. I know something of men. He you call superior, whom I saw for some moments after the shipwreck at Cardoville Castle, has a bad look; and I am sorry to see you enrolled under such a commander."

"At Cardoville Castle!" exclaimed Agricola, struck with the identity of the name with that of the young lady of the golden hair; "was it in Cardoville Castle that you were received after your shipwreck?"

"Yes, my boy; why, does that astonish you?" asked Dagobert.

"Nothing father; but were the owners of the castle there at the time?"

"No; for the steward, when I applied to him for an opportunity to return thanks for the kind hospitality we had experienced, informed me that the person to whom the house belonged was resident at Paris."

"What a singular coincidence," thought Agricola, "if the young lady should be the proprietor of the dwelling which bears her name!"

This reflection having recalled to Agricola the promise which he had made to Mother Bunch, he said to Dagobert; "Dear father, excuse me; but it is already late, and I ought to be in the workshop by eight o'clock."

"That is too true, my boy. Let us go. This party is adjourned till my return from Chartres. Embrace me once more, and take care of yourself."

Since Dagobert had spoken of constraint and oppression to Gabriel, the latter had continued pensive. At the moment when Agricola approached him to shake hands, and to bid him adieu, the missionary said to him solemnly, with a grave voice, and in a tone of decision that astonished both the blacksmith and the soldier: "My dear brother, one word more. I have come here to say to you also that within a few days hence I shall have need of you; and of you also, my father (permit me so to call you),"added Gabriel, with emotion, as he turned round to Dagobert.

"How! you speak thus to us!" exclaimed Agricola; "what is the matter?"

"Yes," replied Gabriel, "I need the advice and assistance of two men of honor - of two men of resolution; - and I can reckon upon you two - can I not? At any hour, on whatever day it may be, upon a word from me, will you come?"

Dagobert and his son regarded each other in silence, astonished at the accents of the missionary. Agricola felt an oppression of the heart. If he should be a prisoner when his brother should require his assistance, what could be done?

"At every hour, by night or by day, my brave boy, you may depend upon us," said Dagobert, as much surprised as interested - "You have a father and a brother; make your own use of them."

"Thanks, thanks," said Gabriel, "you set me quite at ease."

"I'll tell you what," resumed the soldier, "were it not for your priest's robe, I should believe, from the manner in which you have spoken to us, that you are about to be engaged in a duel - in a mortal combat."

"In a duel?" said Gabriel, starting. "Yes; it may be a duel - uncommon and fearful - at which it is necessary to have two witnesses such as you - A FATHER and A BROTHER!"

Some instants afterwards, Agricola, whose anxiety was continually increasing, set off in haste for the dwelling of Mademoiselle de Cardoville, to which we now beg leave to take the reader.

CHAPTER XXXIII

THE PAVILION

Dizier House was one of the largest and handsomest in the Rue Babylone, in Paris. Nothing could be more severe, more imposing, or more depressing than the aspect of this old mansion. Several immense windows, filled with small squares of glass, painted a grayish white, increased the sombre effect of the massive layers of huge stones, blackened by time, of which the fabric was composed.

This dwelling bore a resemblance to all the others that had been erected in the same quarter towards the middle of the last century. It was surmounted in front by a pediment; it had an elevated ground floor, which was reached from the outside by a circular flight of broad stone steps. One of the fronts looked on an immense court-yard, on each side of which an arcade led to the vast interior departments. The other front overlooked the garden, or rather park, of twelve or fifteen roods; and, on this side, wings, approaching the principal part of the structure, formed a couple of lateral galleries. Like nearly all the other great habitations of this quarter, there might be seen at the extremity of the garden, what the owners and occupiers of each called the lesser mansion.

This extension was a Pompadour summer-house, built in the form of a rotunda, with the charming though incorrect taste of the era of its erection. It presented, in every part where it was possible for the stones to be cut, a profusion of endives, knots of ribbons, garlands of flowers, and chubby cupids. This pavilion, inhabited by Adrienne de Cardoville was composed of a ground floor, which was reached by a peristyle of several steps. A small vestibule led to a circular hall, lighted from the roof. Four principal apartments met here; and ranges of smaller rooms, concealed in the upper story, served for minor purposes.

These dependencies of great habitations are in our days disused, or transformed into irregular conservatories; but by an uncommon exception, the black exterior of the pavilion had been scraped and renewed, and the entire structure repaired. The white stones of which it was built glistened like Parian marble; and its renovated, coquettish aspect contrasted singularly with the gloomy mansion seen at the other extremity of an extensive lawn, on which were planted here and there gigantic clumps of verdant trees.

The following scene occurred at this residence on the morning following that of the arrival of Dagobert, with the daughters of Marshal Simon, in the Rue Brise-Miche. The hour of eight had sounded from the steeple of a neighboring church; a brilliant winter sun arose to brighten a pure blue sky behind the tall leafless trees, which in summer formed a dome of verdure over the summer-house. The door in the vestibule opened, and the rays of the morning sun beamed upon a charming creature, or rather upon two charming creatures, for the second one, though filling a modest place in the scale of creation, was not less distinguished by beauty of its own, which was very striking. In plain terms two individuals, one of them a young girl, and the other a tiny English dog, of great beauty, of that breed of spaniels called King Charles's, made their appearance under the peristyle of the rotunda. The name of the young girl was Georgette; the beautiful little spaniel's was Frisky. Georgette was in her eighteenth year. Never had Florine or Manton, never had a lady's maid of Marivaux, a more mischievous face, an eye more quick, a smile more roguish, teeth more white, cheeks more roseate, figure more coquettish, feet smaller, or form smarter, attractive, and enticing. Though it was yet very early, Georgette was carefully and tastefully dressed. A tiny Valenciennes cap, with flaps and flap-band, of half peasant fashion, decked with rose-colored ribbons, and stuck a little backward upon bands of beautiful fair hair, surrounded her fresh and piquant face; a robe of gray levantine, and a cambric neck-kerchief, fastened to her bosom by a large tuft of rose-colored ribbons, displayed her figure elegantly rounded; a hollands apron, white as snow, trimmed below by three large hems, surmounted by a Vandyke-row, encircled her waist, which was as round and flexible as a reed; her short, plain sleeves, edged with bone lace, allowed her plump arms to be seen, which her long Swedish gloves, reaching to the elbow, defended from the rigor of the cold. When Georgette raised the bottom of her dress, in order to descend more quickly the steps, she exhibited to Frisky's indifferent eyes a beautiful ankle, and the beginning of the plump calf of a fine leg, encased in white silk, and a charming little foot, in a laced half-boot of Turkish satin. When a blonde like Georgette sets herself to be ensnaring; when vivid glances sparkle from her eyes of bright yet tender blue; when a joyous excitement suffuses her transparent skin, she is more resistless for the conquest of everything before her than a brunette.

This bewitching and nimble lady's-maid, who on the previous evening had introduced Agricola to the pavilion, was first waiting woman to the Honorable Miss Adrienne de Cardoville, niece of the Princess Saint Dizier.

Frisky, so happily found and brought back by the blacksmith, uttered weak but joyful barks, and bounded, ran, and frolicked upon the turf. She was not much bigger than one's fist; her curled hair, of lustrous black, shone like ebony, under the broad, red satin ribbon which encircled her neck; her paws, fringed with long silken fur, were of a bright and fiery tan, as well as her muzzle, the nose of which was inconceivably pug; her large eyes were full of intelligence; and her curly ears so long that they trailed upon the ground. Georgette seemed to be as brisk and petulant as Frisky, and shared her sportiveness, - now scampering after the happy little spaniel, and now retreating, in order to be pursued upon the greensward in her turn. All at once, at the sight of a second person, who advanced with deliberate gravity, Georgette and Frisky were suddenly stopped in their diversion. The little King Charles, some steps in advance of Georgette, faithful to her name, and bold as the devil, held herself firmly upon her nervous paws, and fiercely awaited the coming up of the enemy, displaying at the same time rows of little teeth, which, though of ivory, were none the less pointed and sharp. The enemy consisted of a woman of mature age, accompanied by a very fat dog, of the color of coffee and milk; his tail was twisted like a corkscrew; he was pot-bellied; his skin was sleek; his neck was turned little to one side; he walked with his legs inordinately spread out, and stepped with the air of a doctor. His black muzzle, quarrelsome and scowling showed two fangs sallying forth, and turning up from the left side of the mouth, and altogether he had an expression singularly forbidding and vindictive. This disagreeable animal, a perfect type of what might be called a "church-goer's pug," answered to the name of "My Lord." His mistress, a woman of about fifty years of age, corpulent and of middle size, was dressed in a costume as gloomy and severe as that of Georgette was gay and showy. It consisted of a brown robe, a black silk mantle, and a hat of the same dye. The features of this woman might have been agreeable in her youth; and her florid cheeks, her correct eyebrows, her black eyes, which were still very lively, scarcely accorded with the peevish and austere physiognomy which she tried to assume. This matron, of slow and discreet gait, was Madame Augustine Grivois, first woman to the Princess Saint-Dizier. Not only did the age, the face, and the dress of these two women present a striking contrast; but the contrast extended itself even to the animals which attended them. There were similar differences between Frisky and My Lord, as between Georgette and Mrs. Grivois. When the latter perceived the little King Charles, she could not restrain a movement of surprise and repugnance, which escaped not the notice of the young lady's maid. Frisky, who had not retreated one inch, since the apparition of My Lord, regarded him valiantly, with a look of defiance, and even advanced towards him with an air so decidedly hostile, that the cur, though thrice as big as the little King Charles, uttered a howl of distress and terror, and sought refuge behind Mrs. Grivois, who bitterly said to Georgette:

"It seems to me, miss, that you might dispense with exciting your dog thus, and setting him upon mine."

"It was doubtless for the purpose of protecting this respectable but ugly animal from similar alarms, that you tried to make us lose Frisky yesterday, by driving her into the street through the little garden gate. But fortunately an honest young man found Frisky in the Rue de Babylone, and brought her back to my mistress. However," continued Georgette, "to what, madame, do I owe the pleasure of seeing you this morning?"

"I am commanded by the Princess," replied Mrs. Grivois, unable to conceal a smile of triumphant satisfaction, "immediately to see Miss Adrienne. It regards a very important affair, which I am to communicate only to herself."

At these words Georgette became purple, and could not repress a slight start of disquietude, which happily escaped Grivois, who was occupied with watching over the safety of her pet, whom Frisky continued to snarl at with a very menacing aspect; and Georgette, having quickly overcome her temporary emotion, firmly answered: "Miss Adrienne went to rest very late last night. She has forbidden me to enter her apartment before mid day."

"That is very possible: but as the present business is to obey an order of the Princess her aunt, you will do well if you please, miss, to awaken your mistress immediately."

"My mistress is subject to no one's orders in her own house; and I will not disturb her till mid-day, in pursuance of her commands," replied Georgette.

"Then I shall go myself," said Mrs. Grivois.

"Florine and Hebe will not admit you. Indeed, here is the key of the saloon; and through the saloon only can the apartments of Miss Adrienne be entered."

"How! do you dare refuse me permission to execute the orders of the Princess?"

"Yes; I dare to commit the great crime of being unwilling to awaken my mistress!"

"Ah! such are the results of the blind affection of the Princess for her niece," said the matron, with affected grief: "Miss Adrienne no longer respects her aunt's orders; and she is surrounded by young hare-brained persons, who, from the first dawn of morning, dress themselves out as if for ball-going."

"Oh, madame! how came you to revile dress, who were formerly the greatest coquette and the most frisky and fluttering of all the Princess's women. At least, that is what is still spoken of you in the hotel, as having been handed down from time out of mind, by generation to generation, even unto ours!"

"How! from generation to generation! do you mean to insinuate that I am a hundred years old, Miss Impertinence?"

"I speak of the generations of waiting-women; for, except you, it is the utmost if they remain two or three years in the Princess's house, who has too many tempers for the poor girls!"

"I forbid you to speak thus of my mistress, whose name some people ought not to pronounce but on their knees."

"However," said Georgette, "if one wished to speak ill of -"

"Do you dare!"

"No longer ago than last night, at half past eleven o'clock -"

"Last night?"

"A four-wheeler," continued Georgette, "stopped at a few paces from the house. A mysterious personage, wrapped up in a cloak, alighted from it, and directly tapped, not at the door, but on the glass of the porter's lodge window; and at one o'clock in the morning, the cab was still stationed in the street, waiting for the mysterious personage in the cloak, who, doubtless, during all that time, was, as you say, pronouncing the name of her Highness the Princess on his knees."

Whether Mrs. Grivois had not been instructed as to a visit made to the Princess Saint-Dizier by Rodin (for he was the man in the cloak), in the middle of the night, after he had become certain of the arrival in Paris of General Simon's daughters; or whether Mrs. Grivois thought it necessary to appear ignorant of the visit, she replied, shrugging her shoulders disdainfully: "I know not what you, mean, madame. I have not come here to listen to your impertinent stuff. Once again I ask you - will you, or will you not, introduce me to the presence of Miss Adrienne?"

"I repeat, madame, that my mistress sleeps, and that she has forbidden me to enter her bed-chamber before mid-day."

This conversation took place at some distance from the summer-house, at a spot from which the peristyle could be seen at the end of a grand avenue, terminating in trees arranged in form of a V. All at once Mrs. Grivois, extending her hand in that direction, exclaimed: "Great heavens! is it possible? what have I seen?"

"What have you seen?" said Georgette, turning round.

"What have I seen?" repeated Mrs. Grivois, with amazement.

"Yes: what was it?"

"Miss Adrienne."

"Where?" asked Georgette.

"I saw her run up the porch steps. I perfectly recognized her by her gait, by her hat, and by her mantle. To come home at eight o'clock in the morning!" cried Mrs. Grivois: "it is perfectly incredible!"

"See my lady? Why, you came to see her!" and Georgette burst out into fits of laughter: and then said: "Oh! I understand! you wish to out-do my story of the four-wheeler last night! It is very neat of you!"

"I repeat," said Mrs. Grivois, "that I have this moment seen -"

"Oh! adone, Mrs. Grivois: if you speak seriously, you are mad!"

"I am mad, am I? because I have a pair of good eyes! The little gate that open's on the street lets one into the quincunx near the pavilion. It is by that door, doubtless, that mademoiselle has re-entered. Oh, what shameful conduct! what will the Princess say to it! Ah! her presentiments have not yet been mistaken. See to what her weak indulgence of her niece's caprices has led her! It is monstrous! - so monstrous, that, though I have seen her with my own eyes, still I can scarcely believe it!"

"Since you've gone so far, ma'am, I now insist upon conducting you into the apartment of my lady, in order that you may convince yourself, by your own senses, that your eyes have deceived you!"

"Oh, you are very cunning, my dear, but not more cunning than I! You propose my going now! Yes, yes, I believe you: you are certain that by this time I shall find her in her apartment!"

"But, madame, I assure you -"

"All that I can say to you is this: that neither you, nor Florine, nor Hebe, shall remain here twenty-four hours. The Princess will put an end to this horrible scandal; for I shall immediately inform her of what has passed. To go out in the night! Re-enter at eight o'clock in the morning! Why, I am all in a whirl! Certainly, if I had not seen it with my own eyes, I could not have believed it! Still, it is only what was to be expected. It will astonish nobody. Assuredly not! All those to whom I am going to relate it, will say, I am quite sure, that it is not at all astonishing! Oh! what a blow to our respectable Princess! What a blow for her!"

Mrs. Grivois returned precipitately towards the mansion, followed by her fat pug, who appeared to be as embittered as herself.

Georgette, active and light, ran, on her part, towards the pavilion, in order to apprise Miss de Cardoville that Mrs. Grivois had seen her, or fancied she had seen her, furtively enter by the little garden gate.

CHAPTER XXXIV

ADRIENNE AT HER TOILET

About an hour had elapsed since Mrs. Grivois had seen or pretended to have seen Adrienne de Cardoville re-enter in the morning the extension of Saint-Dizier House.

It is for the purpose, not of excusing, but of rendering intelligible, the following scenes, that it is deemed necessary to bring out into the light some striking peculiarities in the truly original character of Miss de Cardoville.

This originality consisted in an excessive independence of mind, joined to a natural horror of whatsoever is repulsive or deformed, and to an insatiable desire of being surrounded by everything attractive and beautiful. The painter most delighted with coloring and beauty, the sculptor most charmed by proportions of form, feel not more than Adrienne did the noble enthusiasm which the view of perfect beauty always excites in the chosen favorites of nature.

And it was not only the pleasures of sight which this young lady loved to gratify: the harmonious modulations of song, the melody of instruments, the cadences of poetry, afforded her infinite pleasures; while a harsh voice or a discordant noise made her feel the same painful impression, or one nearly as painful as that which she involuntarily experienced from the sight of a hideous object. Passionately fond of flowers, too, and of their sweet scents, there are some perfumes which she enjoyed equally with the delights of music or those of plastic beauty. It is necessary, alas, to acknowledge one enormity: Adrienne was dainty in her food! She valued more than any one else the fresh pulp of handsome fruit, the delicate savor of a golden pheasant, cooked to a turn, and the odorous cluster of a generous vine.

But Adrienne enjoyed all these pleasures with an exquisite reserve. She sought religiously to cultivate and refine the senses given her. She would have deemed it black ingratitude to blunt those divine gifts by excesses, or to debase them by unworthy selections of objects upon which to exercise them; a fault from which, indeed, she was preserved by the excessive and imperious delicacy of her taste.

The BEAUTIFUL and the UGLY occupied for her the places which GOOD and EVIL holds for others.

Her devotion to grace, elegance, and physical beauty, had led her also to the adoration of moral beauty; for if the expression of a low and bad passion render uncomely the most beautiful countenances, those which are in themselves the most ugly are ennobled, on the contrary, by the expression of good feelings and generous sentiments.

In a word, Adrienne was the most complete, the most ideal personification of SENSUALITY - not of vulgar, ignorant, non intelligent, mistaken sensuousness which is always deceit ful and corrupted by habit or by the necessity for gross and ill-regulated enjoyments, but that exquisite sensuality which is to the senses what intelligence is to the soul.

The independence of this young lady's character was extreme. Certain humiliating subjections imposed upon her success by its social position, above all things were revolting to her, and she had the hardihood to resolve to withdraw herself from them. She was a woman, the most womanish that it is possible to imagine - a woman in her timidity as well as in her audacity - a woman in her hatred of the brutal despotism of men, as well as in her intense disposition to self-devoting herself, madly even and blindly, to him who should merit such a devotion from her - a woman whose piquant wit was occasionally paradoxical - a superior woman, in brief, who entertained a well-grounded disdain and contempt for certain men either placed very high or greatly adulated, whom she had from time to time met in the drawing-room of her aunt, the Princess Saint-Dizier, when she resided with her.

These indispensable explanations being given, we usher, the reader into the presence of Adrienne de Cardoville, who had just come out of the bath.

It would require all the brilliant colorings of the Venetian school to represent that charming scene, which would rather seem to have occurred in the sixteenth century, in some palace of Florence or Bologna, than in Paris, in the Faubourg Saint-Germain, in the month of February, 1832.

Adrienne's dressing-room was a kind of miniature temple seemingly one erected and dedicated to the worship of beauty, in gratitude to the Maker who has lavished so many charms upon woman, not to be neglected by her, or to cover and conceal them with ashes, or to destroy them by the contact of her person with sordid and harsh haircloth; but in order that, with fervent gratitude for the divine gifts wherewith she is endowed, she may enhance her charms with all the illusions of grace and all the splendors of apparel, so as to glorify the divine work of her own perfections in the eyes of all. Daylight was admitted into this semicircular apartment, through one of those double windows, contrived for the preservation of heat, so happily imported from Germany. The walls of the pavilion being constructed of stone of great thickness, the depth of the aperture for the windows was therefore very great. That of Adrienne's dressing-room was closed on the outside by a sash containing a single large pane of plate glass, and within, by another large plate of ground glass. In the interval or space of about three feet left between these two transparent enclosures, there was a case or box filled with furze mould, whence sprung forth climbing plants, which, directed round the ground glass, formed a rich garland of leaves and flowers. A garnet damask tapestry, rich with harmoniously blended arabesques, in the purest style, covered the walls and a thick carpet of similar color was extended over the floor: and this sombre ground, presented by the floor and walls, marvellously enhanced the effects of all the harmonious ornaments and decorations of the chamber.

Under the window, opposite to the south, was placed Adrienne's dressing case, a real masterpiece of the skill of the goldsmith. Upon a large tablet of lapis-lazuli, there were scattered boxes of jewels, their lids precisely enamelled; several scent boxes of rock crystal, and other implements and utensils of the toilet, some formed of shells, some of mother-of-pearl, and others of ivory, covered with ornaments of gold in extraordinary taste. Two large figures, modelled in silver with antique purity; supported an oval swing mirror, which had for its rim, in place of a frame curiously carved, a fresh garland of natural flowers, renewed every day like a nosegay for a ball.

Two enormous Japanese vases, of purple and gold, three feet each in diameter, were placed upon the carpet on each side of the toilet, and, filled with camellias, ibiscures, and cape jasmine, in full flower formed a sort of grove, diversified with the most brilliant colors. At the farther end of the apartment, opposite the casement, was to be seen, surrounded by another mass of flowers, a reduction in white marble of the enchanting group of Daphnis and Chloe, the more chaste ideal of graceful modesty and youthful beauty.

Two golden lamps burned perfumes upon the same pedestal which supported those two charming figures. A coffer of frosted silver, set off with small figures in jewelry and precious stones, and supported on four feet of gilt bronze, contained various necessaries for the toilette; two frosted Psyches, decorated with diamond ear-rings; some excellent drawings from Raphael and Titian, painted by Adrienne herself, consisting of portraits of both men and women of exquisite beauty; several consoles of oriental jasper, supporting ewers and basins of silver and of silver gilt, richly chased and filled with scented waters; a voluptuously rich divan, some seats, and an illuminated gilt fable, completed the furniture of this chamber, the atmosphere of which was impregnated with the sweetest perfumes.

Adrienne, whom her attendants had just helped from the bath, was seated before her toilette, her three women surrounding her. By a caprice, or rather by a necessary and logical impulse of her soul, filled as it was with the love of beauty and of harmony in all things, Adrienne had wished the young women who served her to be very pretty, and be dressed with attention and with a charming originality. We have already seen Georgette, a piquante blonde, attired in her attractive costume of an intriguing lady's maid of Marivaux; and her two companions were quite equal to her both in gracefulness and gentility.

One of them, named Florine, a tall, delicately slender, and elegant girl, with the air and form of Diana Huntress, was of a pale brown complexion. Her thick black hair was turned up behind, where it was fastened with a long golden pin. Like the two other girls, her arms were uncovered to facilitate the performance of her duties about and upon the person of her charming mistress. She wore a dress of that gay green so familiar to the Venetian painters. Her petticoat was very ample. Her slender waist curved in from under the plaits of a tucker of white cambric, plaited in five minute folds, and fastened by five gold buttons. The third of Adrienne's women had a face so fresh and ingenuous, a waist so delicate, so pleasing, and so finished, that her mistress had given her the name of Hebe. Her dress of a delicate rose color, and Grecian cut, displayed her charming neck, and her beautiful arms up to the very shoulders. The physiognomy of these three young women was laughter loving and happy. On their features there was no expression of that bitter sullenness, willing and hated obedience, or offensive familiarity, or base and degraded deference, which are the ordinary results of a state of servitude.

In the zealous eagerness of the cares and attentions which they lavished upon Adrienne, there seemed to be at least as much of affection as of deference and respect. They appeared to derive an ardent pleasure from the services which they rendered to their lovely mistress. One would have thought that they attached to the dressing and embellishment of her person all the merits and the enjoyment arising from the execution of a work of art, in the accomplishing of which, fruitful of delights, they were stimulated by the passions of love, of pride, and of joy.

The sun beamed brightly upon the toilet-case, placed in front of the window. Adrienne was seated on a chair, its back elevated a little more than usual. She was enveloped in a long morning-gown of blue silk, embroidered with a leaf of the same color, which was fitted close to her waist, as exquisitely slender and delicate as that of a child of twelve years, by a girdle with floating tags. Her neck, delicately slender and flexible as a bird's, was uncovered, as were also her shoulders and arms, and all were of incomparable beauty. Despite the vulgarity of the comparison, the purest ivory alone can give an idea of the dazzling whiteness of her polished satin skin, of a texture so fresh and so firm, that some drops of water, collected and still remaining about the roots of her hair from the bath, rolled in serpentine lines over her shoulders, like pearls, or beads, of crystal, over white marble.

And what gave enhanced lustre to this wondrous carnation, known but to auburn-headed beauties, was the deep purple of her, humid lips, - the roseate transparency of her small ears, of her dilated nostrils, and her nails, as bright and glossy, as if they had been varnished. In every spot, indeed, where her pure arterial blood, full of animation and heat, could make its way to the skin and shine through the surface, it proclaimed her high health and the vivid life and joyous buoyancy of her glorious youth. Her eyes were very large, and of a velvet softness. Now they glanced, sparkling and shining with comic humor or intelligence and wit; and now they widened and extended themselves, languishing and swimming between their double fringes of long crisp eyelashes, of as deep a black as her finely-drawn and exquisitely arched eyebrows; for, by a delightful freak of nature, she had black eyebrows and eyelashes to contrast with the golden red of her hair. Her forehead, small like those of ancient Grecian statues, formed with the rest of her face a perfect oval. Her nose, delicately curved, was slightly aquiline; the enamel of her teeth glistened when the light fell upon them; and her vermeil mouth voluptuously sensual, seemed to call for sweet kisses, and the gay smiles and delectations of dainty and delicious pleasure. It is impossible to behold or to conceive a carriage of the head freer, more noble, or more elegant than hers; thanks to the great distance which separated the neck and the ear from their attachment to her outspread and dimpled shoulders. We have already said that Adrienne was red-haired; but it was the redness of many of the admirable portraits of women by Titian and Leonardo da Vinci, - that is to say, molten gold presents not reflections more delightfully agreeable or more glittering, than the naturally undulating mass of her very long hair, as soft and fine as silk, so long, that, when let loose, it reached the floor; in it, she could wholly envelop herself, like another Venus arising from the sea. At the present moment, Adrienne's tresses were ravishing to behold; Georgette, her arms bare, stood behind her mistress, and had carefully collected into one of her small white hands, those splendid threads whose naturally ardent brightness was doubled in the sunshine. When the pretty lady's-maid pulled a comb of ivory into the midst of the undulating and golden waves of that enormously magnificent skein of silk, one might have said that a thousand sparks of fire darted forth and coruscated away from it in all directions. The sunshine, too, reflected not less golden and fiery rays from numerous clusters of spiral ringlets, which, divided upon Adrienne's forehead, fell over her cheeks, and in their elastic flexibility caressed the risings of her snowy bosom, to whose charming undulations they adapted and applied themselves. Whilst Georgette, standing, combed the beautiful locks of her mistress, Hebe, with one knee upon the floor, and having upon the other the sweet little foot of Miss Cardoville, busied herself in fitting it with a remarkably small shoe of black satin, and crossed its slender ties over a silk stocking of a pale yet rosy flesh color, which imprisoned the smallest and finest ankle in the world. Florine, a little farther back, presented to her mistress, in a jeweled box, a perfumed paste, with which Adrienne slightly rubbed her dazzling hands and outspread fingers, which seemed tinted with carmine to their extremities. Let us not forget Frisky, who, couched in the lap of her mistress, opened her great eyes with all her might, and seemed to observe the different operations of Adrienne's toilette with grave and reflective attention. A silver bell being sounded from without, Florine, at a sign from her mistress, went out and presently returned, bearing a letter upon a small silver-gilt salve. Adrienne, while her women continued fitting on her shoes, dressing her hair, and arranging her in her habiliments, took the letter, which was written by the steward of the estate of Cardoville, and read aloud as follows:

"HONORED MADAME,

"Knowing your goodness of heart and generosity, I venture to address you with respectful confidence. During twenty years I served the late Count and Duke of Cardoville, your noble father, I believe I may truly say, with probity and zeal. The castle is now sold; so that I and my wife, in our old age, behold ourselves about to be dismissed, and left destitute of all resources: which, alas! is very hard at our time of life."

"Poor creature!" said Adrienne, interrupting herself in reading: "my father, certainly, always prided himself upon their devotion to him, and their probity." She continued:

"There does, indeed, remain to us a means of retaining our place here; but it would constrain us to be guilty of baseness; and, be the consequences to us what they may, neither I nor my wife wish to purchase our bread at such a price."

"Good, very good," said Adrienne, "always the same - dignity even in poverty - it is the sweet perfume of a flower, not the less sweet because it has bloomed in a meadow."

"In order to explain to you, honored madame, the unworthy task exacted from us, it is necessary to inform you, in the first place, that M. Rodin came here from Paris two days ago."

"Ah! M. Rodin!" said Mademoiselle de Cardoville, interrupting herself anew; "the secretary of Abbe d'Aigrigny! I am not at all surprised at him being engaged in a perfidious or black intrigue. But let us see."

"M. Rodin came from Paris to announce to us that the estate was sold, and that he was sure of being able to obtain our continuance in our place, if we would assist him in imposing a priest not of good character upon the new proprietress as her future confessor; and if, the better to attain this end, we would consent to calumniate another priest, a deserving and excellent man, much loved and much respected in the country. Even that is not all. I was required to write twice or thrice a week to M. Rodin, and to relate to him everything that should occur in the house. I ought to acknowledge, honored madame, that these infamous proposals were as much as possible disguised and dissimulated under sufficiently specious pretexts; but, notwithstanding the aspect which with more or less skill it was attempted to give to the affair, it was precisely and substantially what I have now had the honor of stating to you."

"Corruption, calumny, and false and treacherous impeachment!" said Adrienne, with disgust: "I cannot think of such wretches without involuntarily feeling my mind shocked by dismal ideas of black, venomous, and vile reptiles, of aspects most hideous indeed. How much more do I love to dwell upon the consoling thought of honest Dupont and his wife!" Adrienne proceeded:

"Believe me, we hesitated not an instant. We quit Cardoville, which has been our home for the last twenty years; - but we shall quit it like honest people, and with the consciousness of our integrity. And now, honored madame, if, in the brilliant circle in which you move - you, who are so benevolent and amiable - could find a place for us by your recommendation, then, with endless gratitude to you, we shall escape from a position of most cruel embarrassment."

"Surely, surely," said Adrienne, "they shall not in vain appeal to me. To wrest excellent persons from the grip of M. Rodin, is not only a duty but a pleasure: for it is at once a righteous and a dangerous enterprise; and dearly do I love to brave powerful oppressors!" Adrienne again went on reading:

"After having thus spoken to you of ourselves, honored madame, permit us to implore your protection for other unfortunates; for it would be wicked to think only of one's self. Three days ago, two shipwrecks took place upon our ironbound coast. A few passengers only were saved, and were conducted hither, where I and my wife gave them all necessary attentions. All these passengers have departed for Paris, except one, who still remains, his wounds having hitherto prevented him from leaving the house, and, indeed, they will constrain him to remain for some days to come. He is a young East Indian prince, of about twenty years of age, and he appears to be as amiable and good as he is handsome, which is not a little to say, though he has a tawny skin, like the rest of his countrymen, as I understand."

"An Indian prince! twenty years of age! young, amiable, and handsome!" exclaimed Adrienne, gayly; "this is quite delightful, and not at all of an ordinary or vulgar nature! Oh! this Indian prince has already awakened all my sympathies! But what can I do with this Adonis from the banks of the Ganges, who has come to wreck himself upon the Picardy coast?"

Adrienne's three women looked at her with much astonishment, though they were accustomed to the singular eccentricities of her character.

Georgette and Hebe even indulged in discreet and restrained smiles. Florine, the tall and beautiful pale brown girl, also smiled like her pretty companions; but it was after a short pause of seeming reflection, as if she had previously been entirely engrossed in listening to and recollecting the minutest words of her mistress, who, though powerfully interested by the situation of the "Adonis from Ganges banks," as she had called him, continued to read Dupont's letter:

"One of the countrymen of the Indian prince, who has also remained to attend upon him, has given me to understand that the youthful prince has lost in the shipwreck all he possessed, and knows not how to get to Paris, where his speedy presence is required by some affairs of the very greatest importance. It is not from the prince himself that I have obtained this information: no; he appears to be too dignified and proud to proclaim of his fate: but his countryman, more communicative, confidentially told me what I have stated, adding, that his young compatriot has already been subjected to great calamities, and that his father, who was the sovereign of an Indian kingdom, has been killed by the English, who have also dispossessed his son of his crown."

"This is very singular," said Adrienne, thoughtfully. "These circumstances recall to my mind that my father often mentioned that one of our relations was espoused in India by a native monarch; and that General Simon: (whom they have created a marshal) had entered into his service." Then interrupting herself to indulge in a smile, she added, "Gracious! this affair will be quite odd and fantastical! Such things happen to nobody but me; and then people say that I am the uncommon creature! But it seems to me that it is not I, but Providence, which, in truth, sometimes shows itself very eccentric! But let us see if worthy Dupont gives the name of this handsome prince?"

"We trust, honored madame, that you will pardon our boldness: but we should have thought ourselves very selfish, if, while stating to you our own griefs, we had not also informed you that there is with us a brave and estimable prince involved in so much distress. In fine, lady, trust to me; I am old; and I have had much experience of men; and it was only necessary to see the nobleness of expression and the sweetness of countenance of this young Indian, to enable me to judge that he is worthy of the interest which I have taken the liberty to request in his behalf. It would be sufficient to transmit to him a small sum of money for the purchase of some European clothing; for he has lost all his Indian vestments in the shipwreck."

"Good heavens! European clothing!" exclaimed Adrienne, gayly. "Poor young prince! Heaven preserve him from that; and me also! Chance has sent hither from the heart of India, a mortal so far favored as never to have worn the abominable European costume - those hideous habits, and frightful hats, which render the men so ridiculous, so ugly, that in truth there is not a single good quality to be discovered in them, nor one spark of what can either captivate or attract! There comes to me at last a handsome young prince from the East, where the men are clothed in silk and cashmere. Most assuredly I'll not miss this rare and unique opportunity of exposing myself to a very serious and formidable temptation! No, no! not a European dress for me, though poor Dupont requests it! But the name - the name of this dear prince! Once more, what a singular event is this! If it should turn out to be that cousin from beyond the Ganges! During my childhood, I have heard so much in praise of his royal father! Oh! I shall be quite ravished to give his son the kind reception which he merits!" And then she read on:

"If, besides this small sum, honored madame, you are so kind as to give him, and also his companion, the means of reaching Paris, you will confer a very great service upon this poor young prince, who is at present so unfortunate.

"To conclude, I know enough of your delicacy to be aware that it would perhaps be agreeable to you to afford this succor to the prince without being known as his benefactress; in which case, I beg that you will be pleased to command me; and you may rely upon my discretion. If, on the contrary, you wish to address it directly to himself, his name is, as it has been written for me by his countrymen, Prince Djalma, son of Radja sing,

King of Mundi."

"Djalma!" said Adrienne, quickly, and appearing to call up her recollections, "Radja-sing! Yes - that is it! These are the very names that my father so often repeated, while telling me that there was nothing more chivalric or heroic in the world than the old king, our relation by marriage; and the son has not derogated, it would seem, from that character. Yes, Djalma, Radja-sing - once more, that is it - such names are not so common," she added, smiling, "that one should either forget or confound them with others. This Djalma is my cousin! Brave and good - young and charming! above all, he has never worn the horrid European dress! And destitute of every resource! This is quite ravishing! It is too much happiness at once! Quick, quick let us improvise a pretty fairy tale, of which the handsome and beloved prince shall be the hero! The poor bird of the golden and azure plumage has wandered into our dismal climate; but he will find here, at least, something to remind him of his native region of sunshine and perfumes!" Then, addressing one of her women, she said: "Georgette, take paper and write, my child!" The young girl went to the gilt, illuminated table, which contained materials for writing; and, having seated herself, she said to her mistress: "I await orders."

Adrienne de Cardoville, whose charming countenance was radiant with the gayety of happiness and joy, proceeded to dictate the following letter to a meritorious old painter, who had long since taught her the arts of drawing and designing; in which arts she excelled, as indeed she did in all others:

"MY DEAR TITIAN, MY GOOD VERONESE, MY WORTHY RAPHAEL.

"You can render me a very great service, - and you will do it, I am sure, with that perfect and obliging complaisance by which you are ever distinguished.

"It is to go immediately and apply yourself to the skillful hand who designed my last costumes of the fifteenth century. But the present affair is to procure modern East Indian dresses for a young man - yes, sir - for a young man, - and according to what I imagine of him, I fancy that you can cause his measure to be taken from the Antinous, or rather, from the Indian Bacchus; yes - that will be more likely.

"It is necessary that these vestments be at once of perfect propriety and correctness, magnificently rich, and of the greatest elegance. You will choose the most beautiful stuffs possible; and endeavor, above all things, that they be, or resemble, tissues of Indian manufacture; and you will add to them, for turbans and sashes, six splendid long cashmere shawls, two of them white, two red, and two orange; as nothing suits brown complexions better than those colors.

"This done (and I allow you at the utmost only two or three days), you will depart post in my carriage for Cardoville Manor House, which you know so well. The steward, the excellent Dupont, one of your old friends, will there introduce you to a young Indian Prince, named Djalma; and you will tell that most potent grave, and reverend signior, of another quarter of the globe, that you have come on the part of an unknown friend, who, taking upon himself the duty of a brother, sends him what is necessary to preserve him from the odious fashions of Europe. You will add, that his friend expects him with so much impatience that he conjures him to come to Paris immediately. If he objects that he is suffering, you will tell him that my carriage is an excellent bed-closet; and you will cause the bedding, etc., which it contains, to be fitted up, till he finds it quite commodious. Remember to make very humble excuses for the unknown friend not sending to the prince either rich palanquins, or even, modestly, a single elephant; for alas! palanquins are only to be seen at the opera; and there are no elephants but those in the menagerie, - though this must make us seem strangely barbarous in his eyes.

"As soon as you shall have decided on your departure, perform the journey as rapidly as possible, and bring here, into my house, in the Rue de Babylone (what predestination! that I should dwell in the street of BABYLON, - a name which must at least accord with the ear of an Oriental), - you will bring hither, I say, this dear prince, who is so happy as to have been born in a country of flowers, diamonds, and sun!

"Above all, you will have the kindness, my old and worthy friend, not to be at all astonished at this new freak, and refrain from indulging in extravagant conjectures. Seriously, the choice which I have made of you in this affair, - of you, whom I esteem and most sincerely honor, - is because it is sufficient to say to you that, at the bottom of all this, there is something more than a seeming act of folly."

In uttering these last words, the tone of Adrienne was as serious and dignified as it had been previously comic and jocose. But she quickly resumed, more gayly, dictating to Georgette.

"Adieu, my old friend. I am something like that commander of ancient days, whose heroic nose and conquering chin you have so often made me draw: I jest with the utmost freedom of spirit even in the moment of battle: yes, for within an hour I shall give battle, a pitched battle - to my dear pew-dwelling aunt. Fortunately, audacity and courage never failed me, and I burn with impatience for the engagement with my austere princess.

"A kiss, and a thousand heartfelt recollections to your excellent wife. If I speak of her here, who is so justly respected, you will please to understand, it is to make you quite at ease as to the consequences of this running away with, for my sake, a charming young prince, - for it is proper to finish well where I should have begun, by avowing to you that he is charming indeed!

"Once more, adieu!"

Then, addressing Georgette, said she, "Have you done writing, chit?"

"Yes, madame."

"Oh, add this postscript."

"P.S. - I send you draft on sight on my banker for all expenses. Spare nothing. You know I am quite a grand seigneur. I must use this masculine expression, since your sex have exclusively appropriated to yourselves (tyrants as you are) a term, so significant as it is of noble generosity."

"Now, Georgette," said Adrienne; "bring me an envelope, and the letter, that I may sign it." Mademoiselle de Cardoville took the pen that Georgette presented to her, signed the letter, and enclosed in it an order upon her banker, which was expressed thus:

"Please pay M. Norval, on demand without grace, the sum of money he may require for expenses incurred on my account.

"ADRIENNE DE CARDOVILLE."

During all this scene, while Georgette wrote, Florine and Hebe had continued to busy themselves with the duties of their mistress's toilette, who had put off her morning gown, and was now in full dress, in order to wait upon the princess, her aunt. From the sustained and immovably fixed attention with which Florine had listened to Adrienne's dictating to Georgette her letter to M. Norval, it might easily have been seen that, as was her habit indeed, she endeavored to retain in her memory even the slightest words of her mistress.

"Now, chit," said Adrienne to Hebe, "send this letter immediately to M. Norval."

The same silver bell was again rung from without. Hebe moved towards the door of the dressing-room, to go and inquire what it was, and also to execute the order of her mistress as to the letter. But Florine precipitated herself, so to speak, before her, and so as to prevent her leaving the apartment; and said to Adrienne:

"Will it please my lady for me to send this letter? I have occasion to go to the mansion."

"Go, Florine, then," said Adrienne, "seeing that you wish it. Georgette, seal the letter."

At the end of a second or two, during which Georgette had sealed the letter, Hebe returned.

"Madame," said she, re-entering, "the working-man who brought back Frisky yesterday, entreats you to admit him for an instant. He is very pale, and he appears quite sad."

"Would that he may already have need of me! I should be too happy!" said Adrienne gayly. "Show the excellent young man into the little saloon. And, Florine, despatch this letter immediately."

Florine went out. Miss de Cardoville, followed by Frisky, entered the little reception-room, where Agricola awaited her.

CHAPTER XXXV

THE INTERVIEW

When Adrienne de Cardoville entered the saloon where Agricola expected her, she was dressed with extremely elegant simplicity. A robe of deep blue, perfectly fitted to her shape, embroidered in front with interlacings of black silk, according to the then fashion, outlined her nymph-like figure, and her rounded bosom. A French cambric collar, fastened by a large Scotch pebble, set as a brooch, served her for a necklace. Her magnificent golden hair formed a framework for her fair countenance, with an incredible profusion of long and light spiral tresses, which reached nearly to her waist.

Agricola, in order to save explanations with his father, and to make him believe that he had indeed gone to the workshop of M. Hardy, had been obliged to array himself in his working dress; he had put on a new blouse though, and the collar of his shirt, of stout linen, very white, fell over upon a black cravat, negligently tied; his gray trousers allowed his well polished boots to be seen; and he held between his muscular hands a cap of fine woolen cloth, quite new. To sum up, his blue blouse, embroidered with red, showing off the nervous chest of the young blacksmith, and indicating his robust shoulders, falling down in graceful folds, put not the least constraint upon his free and easy gait, and became him much better than either frock-coat or dress-coat would have done. While awaiting Miss de Cardoville, Agricola mechanically examined a magnificent silver vase, admirably graven. A small tablet, of the same metal, fitted into a cavity of its antique stand, bore the words - "Chased by JEAN MARIE, working chaser, 1831."

Adrienne had stepped so lightly upon the carpet of her saloon, only separated from another apartment by the doors, that Agricola had not perceived the young lady's entrance. He started, and turned quickly round, upon hearing a silver and brilliant voice say to him-"That is a beautiful vase, is it not, sir?"

"Very beautiful, madame," answered Agricola greatly embarrassed.

"You may see from it that I like what is equitable." added Miss de Cardoville, pointing with her finger to the little silver tablet; - "an artist puts his name upon his painting; an author publishes his on the title-page of his book; and I contend that an artisan ought also to have his name connected with his workmanship."

"Oh, madame, so this name?"

"Is that of the poor chaser who executed this masterpiece, at the order of a rich goldsmith. When the latter sold me the vase, he was amazed at my eccentricity, he would have almost said at my injustice, when, after having made him tell me the name of the author of this production, I ordered his name to be inscribed upon it, instead of that of the goldsmith, which had already been affixed to the stand. In the absence of the rich profits, let the artisan enjoy the fame of his skill. Is it not just, sir?"

It would have been impossible for Adrienne to commence the conversation more graciously: so that the blacksmith, already beginning to feel a little more at ease, answered:

"Being a mechanic myself, madame, I cannot but be doubly affected by such a proof of your sense of equity and justice."

"Since you are a mechanic, sir," resumed Adrienne, "I cannot but felicitate myself on having so suitable a hearer. But please to be seated."

With a gesture full of affability, she pointed to an armchair of purple silk embroidered with gold, sitting down herself upon a tete-a-tete of the same materials.

Seeing Agricola's hesitation, who again cast down his eyes with embarrassment, Adrienne, to encourage him, showed him Frisky, and said to him gayly: "This poor little animal, to which I am very much attached, will always afford me a lively remembrance of your obliging complaisance, sir. And this visit seems to me to be of happy augury; I know not what good presentiment whispers to me, that perhaps I shall have the pleasure of being useful to you in some affair."

"Madame," said Agricola, resolutely, "my name is Baudoin: a blacksmith in the employment of M. Hardy, at Pressy, near the city. Yesterday you offered me your purse and I refused it: to-day, I have come to request of you perhaps ten or twenty times the sum that you had generously proposed. I have said thus much all at once, madame, because it causes me the greatest effort. The words blistered my lips, but now I shall be more at ease."

"I appreciate the delicacy of your scruples, sir," said Adrienne; "but if you knew me, you would address me without fear. How much do you require?"

"I do not know, madame," answered Agricola.

"I beg your pardon. You don't know what sum?"

"No madame; and I come to you to request, not only the sum necessary to me, but also information as to what that sum is."

"Let us see, sir," said Adrienne, smiling, "explain this to me. In spite of my good will, you feel that I cannot divine, all at once, what it is that is required."

"Madame, in two words, I can state the truth. I have a food old mother, who in her youth, broke her health by excessive labor, to enable her to bring me up; and not only me, but a poor abandoned child whom she had picked up. It is my turn now to maintain her; and that I have the happiness of doing. But in order to do so, I have only my labor. If I am dragged from my employment, my mother will be without support."

"Your mother cannot want for anything now, sir, since I interest myself for her."

"You will interest yourself for her, madame?" said Agricola.

"Certainly," replied Adrienne.

"But you don't know her," exclaimed the blacksmith.

"Now I do; yes."

"Oh, madame!" said Agricola, with emotion, after a moment's silence. "I understand you. But indeed you have a noble heart. Mother Bunch was right."

"Mother Bunch?" said Adrienne, looking at Agricola with a very surprised air; for what he said to her was an enigma.

The blacksmith, who blushed not for his friends, replied frankly.

"Madame, permit me to explain, to you. Mother Bunch is a poor and very industrious young workwoman, with whom I have been brought up. She is deformed, which is the reason why she is called Mother Bunch. But though, on the one hand, she is sunk, as low as you are highly elevated on the other, yet as regards the heart - as to delicacy - oh, lady, I am certain that your heart is of equal worth with hers! That was at once her own thought, after I had related to her in what manner, yesterday, you had presented me with that beautiful flower."

"I can assure you, sir," said Adrienne, sincerely touched, "that this comparison flatters and honors me more than anything else that you could say to me, - a heart that remains good and delicate, in spite of cruel misfortunes, is so rare a treasure; while it is very easy to be good, when we have youth and beauty, and to be delicate and generous, when we are rich. I accept, then, your comparison; but on condition that you will quickly put me in a situation to deserve it. Pray go on, therefore."

In spite of the gracious cordiality of Miss de Cardoville, there was always observable in her so much of that natural dignity which arises from independence of character, so much elevation of soul and nobleness of sentiment that Agricola, forgetting the ideal physical beauty of his protectress, rather experienced for her the emotions of an affectionate and kindly, though profound respect, which offered a singular and striking contrast with the youth and gayety of the lovely being who inspired him with this sentiment.

"If my mother alone, madame, were exposed to the rigor which I dread. I should not be so greatly disquieted with the fear of a compulsory suspension of my employment. Among poor people, the poor help one another; and my mother is worshipped by all the inmates of our house, our excellent neighbors, who would willingly succor her. But, they themselves are far from being well off; and as they would incur privations by assisting her, their little benefit would still be more painful to my mother than the endurance even of misery by herself. And besides, it is not only for my mother that my exertions are required, but for my father, whom we have not seen for eighteen years, and who has just arrived from Siberia, where he remained during all that time, from zealous devotion to his former general, now Marshal Simon."

"Marshal Simon!" said Adrienne, quickly, with an expression

of much surprise.

"Do you know the marshal, madame?"

"I do not personally know him, but he married a lady of our family."

"What joy!" exclaimed the blacksmith, "then the two young ladies, his daughters, whom my father has brought from Russia, are your relations!"

"Has Marshal Simon two daughters?" asked Adrienne, more and more astonished and interested.

"Yes, madame, two little angels of fifteen or sixteen, and so pretty, so sweet; they are twins so very much alike, as to be mistaken for one another. Their mother died in exile; and the little she possessed having been confiscated, they have come hither with my father, from the depths of Siberia, travelling very wretchedly; but he tried to make them forget so many privations by the fervency of his devotion and his tenderness. My excellent father! you will not believe, madame, that, with the courage of a lion, he has all the love and tenderness of a mother."

"And where are the dear children, sir?" asked Adrienne.

"At our home, madame. It is that which renders my position so very hard; that which has given me courage to come to you; it is not but that my labor would be sufficient for our little household, even thus augmented; but that I am about to be arrested."

"About to be arrested? For what?"

"Pray, madame, have the goodness to read this letter, which has been sent by some one to Mother Bunch."

Agricola gave to Miss de Cardoville the anonymous letter

which had been received by the workwoman.

After having read the letter, Adrienne said to the blacksmith, with surprise, "It appears, sir, you are a poet!"

"I have neither the ambition nor the pretension to be one, madame. Only, when I return to my mother after a day's toil, and often, even while forging my iron, in order to divert and relax my attention, I amuse myself with rhymes, sometimes composing an ode, sometimes a song."

"And your song of the Freed Workman, which is mentioned in this letter, is, therefore, very disaffected - very dangerous?"

"Oh, no, madame; quite the contrary. For myself, I have the good fortune to be employed in the factory of M. Hardy, who renders the condition of his workpeople as happy as that of their less fortunate comrades is the reverse; and I had limited myself to attempt, in favor of the great mass of the working classes, an equitable, sincere, warm, and earnest claim - nothing more. But you are aware, perhaps, Madame, that in times of conspiracy, and commotion, people are often incriminated and imprisoned on very slight grounds. Should such a misfortune befall me, what will become of my mother, my father, and the two orphans whom we are bound to regard as part of our family until the return of their father, Marshal Simon? It is on this account, madame, that, if I remain, I run the risk of being arrested. I have come to you to request you to provide surety for me; so that I should not be compelled to exchange the workshop for the prison, in which case I can answer for it that the fruits of my labor will suffice for all."

"Thank the stars!" said Adrienne, gayly, "this affair will arrange itself quite easily. Henceforth, Mr. Poet, you shall draw your inspirations in the midst of good fortune instead of adversity. Sad muse! But first of all, bonds shall be given for you."

"Oh, madame, you have saved us!"

"To continue," said Adrienne, "the physician of our family is intimately connected with a very important minister (understand that, as you like," said she, smiling, "you will not deceive yourself much). The doctor exercises very great influence over this great statesman; for he has always had the happiness of recommending to him, on account of his health; the sweets and repose of private life, to the very eve of the day on which his portfolio was taken from him. Keep yourself, then, perfectly at ease. If the surety be insufficient, we shall be able to devise some other means.

"Madame," said Agricola, with great emotion, "I am indebted to you for the repose, perhaps for the life of my mother. Believe that I shall ever be grateful."

"That is all quite simple. Now for another thing. It is proper that those who have too much should have the right of coming to the aid of those who have too little. Marshal Simon's daughters are members of my family, and they will reside here with me, which will be more suitable. You will apprise your worthy mother of this; and in the evening, besides going to thank her for the hospitality which she has shown to my young relations, I shall fetch them home."

At this moment Georgette, throwing open the door which separated the room from an adjacent apartment, hurriedly entered, with an affrighted look, exclaiming:

"Oh, madame, something extraordinary is going on in the street."

"How so? Explain yourself," said Adrienne.

"I went to conduct my dressmaker to the little garden-gate," said Georgette; "where I saw some ill-looking men, attentively examining the walls and windows of the little out-building belonging to the pavilion, as if they wished to spy out some one."

"Madame," said Agricola, with chagrin, "I have not been deceived. They are after me."

"What say you?"

"I thought I was followed, from the moment when I left the Rue St. Merry: and now it is beyond doubt. They must have seen me enter your house; and are on the watch to arrest me. Well, now that your interest has been acquired for my mother, - now that I have no farther uneasiness for Marshal Simon's daughters, - rather than hazard your exposure to anything the least unpleasant, I run to deliver myself up."

"Beware of that sir," said Adrienne, quickly. "Liberty is too precious to be voluntarily sacrificed. Besides, Georgette may have been mistaken. But in any case, I entreat you not to surrender yourself. Take my advice, and escape being arrested. That, I think, will greatly facilitate my measures; for I am of opinion that justice evinces a great desire to keep possession of those upon whom she has once pounced."

"Madame," said Hebe, now also entering with a terrified look, "a man knocked at the little door, and inquired if a young man in a blue blouse has not entered here. He added, that the person whom he seeks is named Agricola Baudoin, and that he has something to tell him of great importance."

"That's my name," said Agricola; "but the important information is a trick to draw me out."

"Evidently," said Adrienne; "and therefore we must play off trick for trick. What did you answer, child?" added she, addressing herself to Hebe.

"I answered, that I didn't know what he was talking about."

"Quite right," said Adrienne: "and the man who put the question?"

"He went away, madame."

"Without doubt to come back again, soon," said Agricola.

"That is very probable," said Adrienne, "and therefore, sir, it is necessary for you to remain here some hours with resignation. I am unfortunately obliged to go immediately to the Princess Saint-Dizier, my aunt, for an important interview, which can no longer be delayed, and is rendered more pressing still by what you have told me concerning the daughters of Marshal Simon. Remain here, then, sir; since if you go out, you will certainly be arrested."

"Madame, pardon my refusal; but I must say once more that I ought not to accept this generous offer."

"Why?"

"They have tried to draw me out, in order to avoid penetrating with the power of the law into your dwelling but if I go not out, they will come in; and never will I expose you to anything so disagreeable. Now that I am no longer uneasy about my mother, what signifies prison?"

"And the grief that your mother will feel, her uneasiness, and her fears, - nothing? Think of your father; and that poor work-woman who loves you as a brother, and whom I value as a sister; - say, sir, do you forget them also? Believe me, it is better to spare those torments to your family. Remain here; and before the evening I am certain, either by giving surety, or some other means, of delivering you from these annoyances."

"But, madame, supposing that I do accept your generous offer, they will come and find me here."

"Not at all. There is in this pavilion, which was formerly the abode of a nobleman's left-handed wife, - you see, sir," said Adrienne, smiling, "that live in a very profane place - there is here a secret place of concealment, so wonderfully well-contrived, that it can defy all searches. Georgette will conduct you to it. You will be very well accommodated. You will even be able to write some verses for me, if the place inspire you."

"Oh, madame! how great is your goodness! how have I merited it?"

"Oh, sir, I will tell you. Admitting that your character and your position do not entitle you to any interest; - admitting that I may not owe a sacred debt to your father for the touching regards and cares he has bestowed upon the daughters of Marshal Simon, my relations - do you forget Frisky, sir?" asked Adrienne, laughing, - "Frisky, there, whom you have restored to my fondles? Seriously, if I laugh," continued this singular and extravagant creature, "it is because I know that you are entirely out of danger, and that I feel an increase of happiness. Therefore, sir, write for me quickly your address, and your mother's, in this pocket-book; follow Georgette; and spin me some pretty verses, if you do not bore yourself too much in that prison to which you fly."

While Georgette conducted the blacksmith to the hiding-place, Hebe brought her mistress a small gray beaver hat with a gray feather; for Adrienne had to cross the park to reach the house occupied by the Princess Saint-Dizier.

A quarter of an hour after this scene, Florine entered mysteriously the apartment of Mrs. Grivois, the first woman of the princess.

"Well?" demanded Mrs. Grivois of the young woman.

"Here are the notes which I have taken this morning," said Florine, putting a paper into the duenna's hand. "Happily, I have a good memory."

"At what time exactly did she return home this morning?" asked the duenna, quickly.

"Who, madame?"

"Miss Adrienne."

"She did not go out, madame. We put her in the bath at nine o'clock."

"But before nine o'clock she came home, after having passed the night out of her house. Eight o'clock was the time at which she returned, however."

Florine looked at Mrs. Grivois with profound astonishment, and said-"I do not understand you, madame."

"What's that? Madame did not come home this morning at eight o'clock? Dare you lie?"

"I was ill yesterday, and did not come down till nine this morning, in order to assist Georgette and Hebe help our young lady from the bath. I know nothing of what passed previously, I swear to you, madame."

"That alters the case. You must ferret out what I allude to from your companions. They don't distrust you, and will tell you all."

"Yes, madame."

"What has your mistress done this morning since you saw her?"

"Madame dictated a letter to Georgette for M. Norval, I requested permission to send it off, as a pretext for going out, and for writing down all I recollected."

"Very well. And this letter?"

"Jerome had to go out, and I gave it him to put in the post-office."

"Idiot!" exclaimed Mrs. Grivois: "couldn't you bring it to me?"

"But, as madame dictated it aloud to Georgette, as is her custom, I knew the contents of the letter; and I have written it in my notes."

"That's not the same thing. It is likely there was need to delay sending off this letter; the princess will be very much displeased."

"I thought I did right, madame."

"I know that it is not good will that fails you. For these six months I have been satisfied with you. But this time you have committed a very great mistake."

"Be indulgent, madame! what I do is sufficiently painful!" The girl stifled a sigh.

Mrs. Grivois looked fixedly at her, and said in a sardonic tone:

"Very well, my dear, do not continue it. If you have scruples, you are free. Go your way."

"You well know that I am not free, madame," said Florine, reddening; and with tears in her eyes she added: "I am dependent upon M. Rodin, who placed me here."

"Wherefore these regrets, then?"

"In spite of one's self, one feels remorse. Madame is so good, and so confiding."

"She is all perfection, certainly! But you are not here to sing her praises. What occurred afterwards?"

"The working-man who yesterday found and brought back Frisky, came early this morning and requested permission to speak with my young lady."

"And is this working-man still in her house?"

"I don't know. He came in when I was going out with the letter."

"You must contrive to learn what it was this workingman came about."

"Yes, madame."

"Has your mistress seemed preoccupied, uneasy, or afraid of the interview which she is to have to-day with the princess? She conceals so little of what she thinks, that you ought to know."

"She has been as gay as usual. She has even jested about the interview!"

"Oh! jested, has she?" said the tire-woman, muttering between her teeth, without Florine being able to hear her: "'They laugh most who laugh last.' In spite of her audacious and diabolical character, she would tremble, and would pray for mercy, if she knew what awaits her this day." Then addressing Florine, she continued-"Return, and keep yourself, I advise you, from those fine scruples, which will be quite enough to do you a bad turn. Do not forget!"

"I cannot forget that I belong not to myself, madame."

"Anyway, let it be so. Farewell."

Florine quitted the mansion and crossed the park to regain the summer house, while Mrs Grivois went immediately to the Princess Saint-Dizier.

Choose from Thousands of 1stWorldLibrary Classics By

A. M. Barnard
Ada Leverson
Adolphus William Ward
Aesop
Agatha Christie
Alexander Aaronsohn
Alexander Kielland
Alexandre Dumas
Alfred Gatty
Alfred Ollivant
Alice Duer Miller
Alice Turner Curtis
Alice Dunbar
Allen Chapman
Ambrose Bierce
Amelia E. Barr
Amory H. Bradford
Andrew Lang
Andrew McFarland Davis
Andy Adams
Anna Alice Chapin
Anna Sewell
Annie Besant
Annie Hamilton Donnell
Annie Payson Call
Annie Roe Carr
Annonaymous
Anton Chekhov
Arnold Bennett
Arthur Conan Doyle
Arthur M. Winfield
Arthur Ransome
Arthur Schnitzler
Atticus
B.H. Baden-Powell
B. M. Bower
B. C. Chatterjee
Baroness Emmuska Orczy
Baroness Orczy
Basil King
Bayard Taylor
Ben Macomber
Bertha Muzzy Bower
Bjornstjerne Bjornson
Booth Tarkington
Boyd Cable
Bram Stoker
C. Collodi
C. E. Orr
C. M. Ingleby
Carolyn Wells
Catherine Parr Traill
Charles A. Eastman
Charles Amory Beach
Charles Dickens
Charles Dudley Warner
Charles Farrar Browne
Charles Ives
Charles Kingsley
Charles Klein
Charles Hanson Towne
Charles Lathrop Pack
Charles Romyn Dake
Charles Whibley
Charles Willing Beale
Charlotte M. Braeme
Charlotte M. Yonge
Charlotte Perkins Stetson
Clair W. Hayes
Clarence Day Jr.
Clarence E. Mulford
Clemence Housman
Confucius
Coningsby Dawson
Cornelis DeWitt Wilcox
Cyril Burleigh
D. H. Lawrence
Daniel Defoe
David Garnett
Dinah Craik
Don Carlos Janes
Donald Keyhoe
Dorothy Kilner
Dougan Clark
Douglas Fairbanks
E. Nesbit
E.P.Roe
E. Phillips Oppenheim
Earl Barnes
Edgar Rice Burroughs
Edith Van Dyne
Edith Wharton
Edward Everett Hale
Edward J. O'Biren
Edward S. Ellis
Edwin L. Arnold
Eleanor Atkins
Eliot Gregory
Elizabeth Gaskell
Elizabeth McCracken
Elizabeth Von Arnim
Ellem Key
Emerson Hough
Emilie F. Carlen
Emily Dickinson
Enid Bagnold
Enilor Macartney Lane
Erasmus W. Jones
Ernie Howard Pie
Ethel May Dell
Ethel Turner
Ethel Watts Mumford
Eugenie Foa
Eugene Wood
Eustace Hale Ball
Evelyn Everett-green
Everard Cotes
F. H. Cheley
F. J. Cross
F. Marion Crawford
Federick Austin Ogg
Ferdinand Ossendowski
Francis Bacon
Francis Darwin
Frances Hodgson Burnett
Frances Parkinson Keyes
Frank Gee Patchin
Frank Harris
Frank Jewett Mather
Frank L. Packard
Frank V. Webster
Frederic Stewart Isham
Frederick Trevor Hill
Frederick Winslow Taylor
Friedrich Kerst
Friedrich Nietzsche
Fyodor Dostoyevsky
G.A. Henty
G.K. Chesterton
Gabrielle E. Jackson
Garrett P. Serviss
Gaston Leroux
George A. Warren
George Ade
Geroge Bernard Shaw
George Durston
George Ebers

George Eliot
George Gissing
George MacDonald
George Meredith
George Orwell
George Sylvester Viereck
George Tucker
George W. Cable
George Wharton James
Gertrude Atherton
Gordon Casserly
Grace E. King
Grace Gallatin
Grace Greenwood
Grant Allen
Guillermo A. Sherwell
Gulielma Zollinger
Gustav Flaubert
H. A. Cody
H. B. Irving
H.C. Bailey
H. G. Wells
H. H. Munro
H. Irving Hancock
H. Rider Haggard
H. W. C. Davis
Haldeman Julius
Hall Caine
Hamilton Wright Mabie
Hans Christian Andersen
Harold Avery
Harold McGrath
Harriet Beecher Stowe
Harry Castlemon
Harry Coghill
Harry Houidini
Hayden Carruth
Helent Hunt Jackson
Helen Nicolay
Hendrik Conscience
Hendy David Thoreau
Henri Barbusse
Henrik Ibsen
Henry Adams
Henry Ford
Henry Frost
Henry James
Henry Jones Ford
Henry Seton Merriman
Henry W Longfellow
Herbert A. Giles
Herbert Carter
Herbert N. Casson
Herman Hesse
Hildegard G. Frey
Homer
Honore De Balzac
Horace B. Day
Horace Walpole
Horatio Alger Jr.
Howard Pyle
Howard R. Garis
Hugh Lofting
Hugh Walpole
Humphry Ward
Ian Maclaren
Inez Haynes Gillmore
Irving Bacheller
Isabel Hornibrook
Israel Abrahams
Ivan Turgenev
J.G.Austin
J. Henri Fabre
J. M. Barrie
J. Macdonald Oxley
J. S. Fletcher
J. S. Knowles
J. Storer Clouston
Jack London
Jacob Abbott
James Allen
James Andrews
James Baldwin
James Branch Cabell
James DeMille
James Joyce
James Lane Allen
James Lane Allen
James Oliver Curwood
James Oppenheim
James Otis
James R. Driscoll
Jane Austen
Jane L. Stewart
Janet Aldridge
Jens Peter Jacobsen
Jerome K. Jerome
John Burroughs
John Cournos
John F. Kennedy
John Gay
John Glasworthy
John Habberton
John Joy Bell
John Kendrick Bangs
John Milton
John Philip Sousa
Jonas Lauritz Idemil Lie
Jonathan Swift
Joseph A. Altsheler
Joseph Carey
Joseph Conrad
Joseph E. Badger Jr
Joseph Hergesheimer
Joseph Jacobs
Jules Vernes
Julian Hawthrone
Julie A Lippmann
Justin Huntly McCarthy
Kakuzo Okakura
Kenneth Grahame
Kenneth McGaffey
Kate Langley Bosher
Kate Langley Bosher
Katherine Cecil Thurston
Katherine Stokes
L. A. Abbot
L. T. Meade
L. Frank Baum
Latta Griswold
Laura Dent Crane
Laura Lee Hope
Laurence Housman
Lawrence Beasley
Leo Tolstoy
Leonid Andreyev
Lewis Carroll
Lewis Sperry Chafer
Lilian Bell
Lloyd Osbourne
Louis Hughes
Louis Tracy
Louisa May Alcott
Lucy Fitch Perkins
Lucy Maud Montgomery
Luther Benson
Lydia Miller Middleton
Lyndon Orr
M. Corvus
M. H. Adams
Margaret E. Sangster
Margret Howth
Margaret Vandercook

Margret Penrose
Maria Edgeworth
Maria Thompson Daviess
Mariano Azuela
Marion Polk Angellotti
Mark Overton
Mark Twain
Mary Austin
Mary Catherine Crowley
Mary Cole
Mary Hastings Bradley
Mary Roberts Rinehart
Mary Rowlandson
M. Wollstonecraft Shelley
Maud Lindsay
Max Beerbohm
Myra Kelly
Nathaniel Hawthrone
Nicolo Machiavelli
O. F. Walton
Oscar Wilde
Owen Johnson
P.G. Wodehouse
Paul and Mabel Thorne
Paul G. Tomlinson
Paul Severing
Percy Brebner
Peter B. Kyne
Plato
R. Derby Holmes
R. L. Stevenson
R. S. Ball
Rabindranath Tagore
Rahul Alvares
Ralph Bonehill
Ralph Henry Barbour
Ralph Victor
Ralph Waldo Emmerson
Rene Descartes
Rex Beach
Rex E. Beach
Richard Harding Davis
Richard Jefferies
Richard Le Gallienne
Robert Barr
Robert Frost
Robert Gordon Anderson
Robert L. Drake
Robert Lansing
Robert Lynd
Robert Michael Ballantyne
Robert W. Chambers
Rosa Nouchette Carey
Rudyard Kipling
Samuel B. Allison
Samuel Hopkins Adams
Sarah Bernhardt
Sarah C. Hallowell
Selma Lagerlof
Sherwood Anderson
Sigmund Freud
Standish O'Grady
Stanley Weyman
Stella Benson
Stella M. Francis
Stephen Crane
Stewart Edward White
Stijn Streuvels
Swami Abhedananda
Swami Parmananda
T. S. Ackland
T. S. Arthur
The Princess Der Ling
Thomas A. Janvier
Thomas A Kempis
Thomas Anderton
Thomas Bailey Aldrich
Thomas Bulfinch
Thomas De Quincey
Thomas Dixon
Thomas H. Huxley
Thomas Hardy
Thomas More
Thornton W. Burgess
U. S. Grant
Valentine Williams
Various Authors
Vaughan Kester
Victor Appleton
Victoria Cross
Virginia Woolf
Wadsworth Camp
Walter Camp
Walter Scott
Washington Irving
Wilbur Lawton
Wilkie Collins
Willa Cather
Willard F. Baker
William Dean Howells
William le Queux
W. Makepeace Thackeray
William W. Walter
William Shakespeare
Winston Churchill
Yei Theodora Ozaki
Yogi Ramacharaka
Young E. Allison
Zane Grey

www.ingramcontent.com/pod-product-compliance
Lightning Source LLC
LaVergne TN
LVHW091640100826
845152LV00006B/106/J

* 9 7 8 1 4 2 1 8 2 3 7 1 3 *